Mind Hacking

Learn How to Banish Negative Thoughts by Boosting Your Ability to Make Sound Decisions through Sharpen Your Mental Focus and Release Your Full Potential (2022 Guide for Beginners)

Archer Howell

Table of Content

INTRODUCTION

Imagine meeting a stranger, and then finding out shortly after that they know you better than your father, your life partner, or your closest friends—possibly even better than you know yourself. You two seem to have been together for your entire life.

What is your genuine self-capable of telling this strange but so familiar person? He is aware of everything you do, including your darkest secrets, and he has an intimate understanding of your innermost feelings that only you possess. You are astounded by how much this individual knows about you and are drawn to his charisma.

The secret is to go inside the subconscious. Some people can find the word to be exceedingly cruel. However, mind hacking is a more advanced form of communication that uses understanding, human knowledge, and empathy to decipher the ideas of the business partner. Additionally, mind control is neither a paranormal practice nor a magic trick.

Contrarily, mind hacking combines psychological knowledge with mentalist expertise intending to learn more about the motivations and attitudes of business partners, earn their trust and loyalty, and ultimately streamline the business. Wouldn't it be helpful if we could immediately develop trust in strangers and if they believed what we believed? What if we knew who's feelings might influence your decision-making? If we can decipher their true wants, intentions, and thoughts?

These are only a few instances of what makes Mind Hacking possible and what incredible outcomes can be attained. Making an effect and paying attention is sometimes necessary for business. Yes, what could be more powerful than demonstrating that you fully understand his thoughts, motivations, and desires? They can open up as long as you enter the same mental space as them. We achieve unanimity and unity in this way. We all enjoy receiving praise and admiration. Furthermore, nobody wants to conduct business with someone they dislike.

The ability to "connect well" with others can be crucial for the job. Whether it's in business meetings, in the office, in the kitchen, or at a company party, private topics are frequently discussed in personal life. One may be considering their family, a pastime, or forthcoming holidays.

It would be easier for anyone whose manager, supervisor, client, or business partner is a good person. Due to the partnership-based nature of Mind Hacking, this is an area where you can succeed. By using Mind Hacking, you can show others that you care about them, want to engage with them, and want to respond to them. Many mind-hacking techniques, which mimic even the smallest expression, seem nearly mundane to use. Even if the other person's feelings are occasionally obvious, you shouldn't be hesitant to express them. By putting the other person's thoughts into words, mind hacking, therefore, has the effect that it does. Mind hacking is simple to use and learn. Because it is based on the typical thought and behavior patterns of men, it is understandable to everyone. Many people would think I was being taken advantage of.

An attitude of hacking is like a knife. It can be used to hurt humans or cut up plants. Therefore, if a user misuses the resources that have been given to him, it is always his fault. I concur that hacking contact should only be utilized in fair win-win situations, that is, in situations when everyone will benefit. When used following their intended purposes, the methods are perfectly acceptable.

You can now anticipate fresh insights emerging from the mentalists' idea bank. I do not doubt that using mind hacking in interviews, lectures, and seminars, as well as in regular interactions, will be quite effective.

WHAT DOES MIND HACKING MEAN?

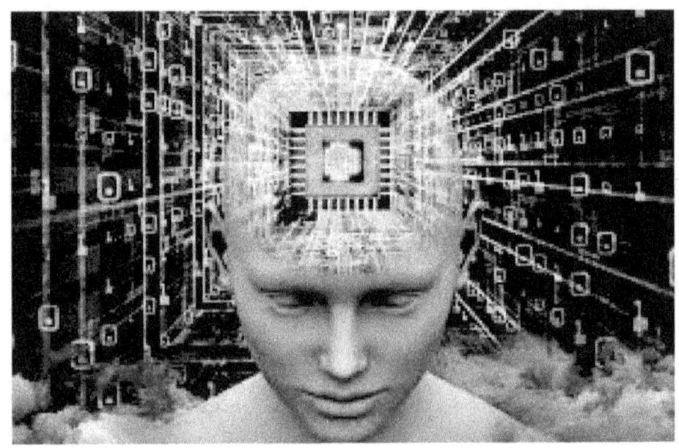

The term "hacking" has a terrible connotation in popular culture. We use it to describe people whose primary means of attack are computer systems or networks. However, the term "hack" is used to describe a creative technique to complete a task or a "quick and dirty" solution to a problem by those who write code. And the term "hacker" is used to describe someone who is "creative" and has the technological know-how to make things happen.

The Hacks exhibition is an effort to reclaim the term, document positive hacking behaviors, and spread the hacker ethos of creative engagement to the general public. Observing how others use new technology to run programs and solve issues is frequently the greatest way to learn about it. The brain is the ideal real estate for potential hackers, much like other secret networks. We can partially satiate this desire because of recent developments in cognitive neuroscience, which illuminate the inner workings of the brain and provide rational explanations for psychological effects rather than merely pointing out their causes. It's impossible to not be interested in how the brain works when viewed from the outside in this way. Other shortcuts result in anomalies in our brains that we can control in unanticipated ways; learning to navigate this recently exposed technology around the kinks entails doing this.

Mind hacking is intended for those who are curious about what is happening inside their heads and for those who want to combine hacks in novel ways to explore the relationship between the self and the world. Engaging is amazingly simple. After all, we all have hearts.

Discover the Mechanisms of the Brain without Peering Inside
The study of fundamental mental functions, such as vision, concentration, memory, language, and decision-making, is known as cognitive psychology. What are the fundamental mind-based operations, the article asks? The problem is that although you can roughly define what someone is doing (the output) and what they are thinking (the input), this doesn't tell you anything about what is happening in between. It is a black box and a typical reverse engineering scenario. Without looking at the code, how are we supposed to comprehend how this works?

Today, of course, we can peek inside the ear using neuroimaging techniques like EEG, PET, and fMRI, or we can use data from brain-damaged individuals regarding anatomy and knowledge to determine how we think the brain is thought to be controlling mental processes.

However, this kind of job was never convenient, simple, or inexpensive. Experimental psychologists have spent more than a century perfecting methods to understand the mind's operations without meddling with the inside; these methods are now referred to as cognitive psychology.

Technically speaking, biological systems are frequently dynamic and occasionally even unpredictable. It implies that there isn't always a one-to-one link between how different data affects the output. In a logical or linear system, the causes and consequences are obvious to discern. However, there is no structured visualization of this in the subconscious. Small things can have tremendous effects, yet often significant changes in the environment don't change how we behave immediately.

Numerous pathways have an impact on biological processes like cognition. It implies that they are adaptable to changes in just one supportive mechanism, but it also implies that they occasionally behave differently when you try to affect them. People lack the consistency that typical apps or computers do. Uncertainty can be attributed to noise and learning.

We don't always respond to the same stimuli in the same manner. We refer to it as the chaos of randomness since it occasionally happens for no apparent reason. For example, when you first get a new bike, you're hesitant at first with your stopping distance, but every time you stop unexpectedly, you're better informed about how to handle its next braking.

However, sometimes our responses change for a reason, not because of noise, and that's because the very act of first-time responding provides input it informs our response pattern for the next time. Since almost all actions affect how a person will think in the future, psychologists make sure that the subject of their studies has either never done the action in issue or has never done it previously.

When people express their opinions on why they did something or how they did it, you can't believe them, which is the problem with trying to imagine how the mind operates. Introspection was a key component of psychology at the start of the twentieth century, and the disagreement it generated helped shape the behaviorism tendency that dominated psychology up until the 1970s.

Behaviorism urged us to limit our consideration of psychology to that which can be correctly assessed and to ignore any ties to interior processes. They were just meant to act as though the study of the relationship between inputs and outcomes in psychology was all there was to it.

Due to this, behavioral psychology became considerably more organized (although some would say less interesting). While cognitive psychologists continue the warm introspection of behaviorists, psychology today recognizes the need to present the mind as more than just a matching of stimulus-response. No more fortunate than anything else they have considered and no more likely to be right is the fact that you believe you have accomplished it.

With us, cognitive psychology has a big impact. The precision and rigor of the methods created by cognitive psychology are still crucial, but they can now be employed in conjunction with methods that shed light on the fundamental makeup of the brain and the mechanisms behind the events under study.

Cognitive behavioral therapy: what is it?

Cognitive behavioral therapy (CBT) is a type of psychotherapy care that aids in helping patients comprehend the ideas and emotions that influence their behavior. Many other disorders, such as phobias, addictions, sleeplessness, and anxiety, are frequently treated with CBT. Typically, cognitive behavioral therapy is brief and concentrated on assisting clients in resolving a very particular issue. Throughout treatment, patients learn how to identify and change damaging or unpleasant thought patterns that negatively affect their actions and emotions.

Basics of Cognitive Behavioral Therapy

The primary idea of CBT is that our ideas and feelings are fundamental to how we behave. As an illustration, someone who spends a lot of time thinking about plane crashes, runway collisions, and other air calamities could decide to forego flying. Cognitive behavioral therapy has grown in popularity over the past few years among mental health consumers and clinicians.

In addition to being scientifically validated and having been found to successfully assist patients in resolving a wide range of maladaptive behaviors, CBT is also frequently more affordable than some other types of treatment because it is typically a choice for short-term care. Automatically having bad thoughts, reducing unconscious negative beliefs that can cause and exacerbate mental health issues, stress, and anxiety is one of the cognitive behavioral therapy's key goals. Such unfavorable ideas arise out of nowhere, are believed to be true, and seem to have a detrimental impact on the victim's disposition.

During the CBT process, patients address these concepts and are encouraged to look for evidence from experience that either supports or contradicts their feelings. People can then approach the emotions that cause their feelings of anxiety and sadness from a more logical and pragmatic standpoint. People may start to engage in more wholesome thought patterns by becoming aware of the unfavorable and frequently unrealistic beliefs that damper their emotions and moods.

Cognitive behavioral therapy types
According to the British Association of Behavioral and Cognitive Psychotherapies, "Cognitive and behavioral psychotherapies are a set of treatments focusing on ideas and values coming from clinical models of human experience and behavior." These cover a broad variety of

treatment options for emotional illnesses, from professional individual psychotherapy to self-help books.

CBT is one of several particular types of therapeutic approaches that are frequently employed by mental health professionals. These sources consist of:

Rational Emotive Behavioral Therapy (REBT)

The main focus of CBT's approach is identifying and changing illogical beliefs. The REBT approach entails identifying fundamentally irrational ideas, vigorously challenging those beliefs, and ultimately learning to comprehend and modify these thought patterns.

Cognitive Therapy

This type of treatment focuses on identifying and changing incorrect or distorted mental, emotional, and behavioral processes.

Multimodal Therapy

According to the cognitive behavioral therapy (CBT) approach, psychological problems should be handled by talking about seven distinct but related modalities, including behavior, consequence, feeling, vision, perception, behavioral influences, and drug/biologic implications.

Dialectical Behavior Treatment

This type of cognitive-behavioral therapy looks at learning habits and attitudes and incorporates skills like emotional control and concentration. Although each cognitive-behavioral treatment strategy has its special characteristics, they all center on addressing the underlying thought patterns that cause psychological suffering.

Cognitive Behavior Therapy's Elements

Sometimes people experience ideas or emotions that support false beliefs or link them together. These convictions may contribute to bad habits that negatively affect families, romantic relationships, jobs, and education, among other aspects of life. For instance, a person with poor self-esteem could harbor unfavorable opinions of their skills or attractiveness. These unfavorable mental patterns may cause the person to continue avoiding social situations or to pass up possibilities for professional or academic growth.

To combat these harmful thoughts and behaviors, a cognitive-behavioral therapist works by assisting the client in identifying the underlying beliefs. The functional analysis level is crucial for understanding how perceptions, feelings, and environmental factors can result in unhelpful behavior. Therapy can be challenging, especially for those who struggle with introspection, but it can eventually result in self-awareness and observations that are crucial to the healing process.

Cognitive behavior therapy's second phase focuses on the underlying behaviors that contributed to the issue. The person keeps picking up new abilities as they are applied in real-world scenarios and practices them. For instance, a drug user can continue to develop new coping mechanisms and practice avoiding or interacting with social circumstances that might otherwise lead to relapse.

The majority of the time, CBT requires a patient to make small, progressive efforts toward a behavior modification. A person with social anxiety may begin by merely visualizing themselves in a setting that makes them uncomfortable. First, the person will keep having dialogues with coworkers, family members, and friends. The cycle gets less difficult and the goals are simpler to accomplish when one advances steadily toward a bigger aim.

Cognitive Behavior Therapy: The Process

During the CBT phase, the psychiatrist typically takes a highly active role. The client and therapist collaborate to achieve the goals that are set by mutual understanding in CBT, which is strongly goal-oriented and client-centered. The client will frequently be given activities to complete between meetings and the psychiatrist will typically give a thorough explanation of the procedure.

Cognitive-behavioral therapy is typically employed as a brief strategy aimed at helping the client resolve a very particular problem.

Cognitive behavior therapy applications

Anxiety, phobias, depression, addictions, eating disorders, panic attacks, post-traumatic stress disorder (PTSD), generalized anxiety disorder (GAD), insomnia, obsessive-compulsive disorder (OCD), substance use disorders, bipolar disorders, schizophrenia, sexual disorders, and childhood depression have all been treated with cognitive behavioral therapy.

Borderline personality disorder; anger; marital strife; substance misuse and addiction; dental phobia; many other mental and physical disorders.

CBT is a helpful method for dealing with emotional difficulties. Could be useful to you, for instance:

Manage mental illness symptoms, prevent mental illness effects from happening, control mental illness when using medicines isn't an option, and learn coping mechanisms for difficult situations.

- Recognize effective coping mechanisms;
- Resolve interpersonal conflicts and improve communication;
- Handle loss or death;
- Overcome bullying or violence-related emotional trauma.
- Control severe illness;
- Control persistent physical symptoms

CBT is one of the most researched intervention kinds, in part because performance can be very simply measured, and care is based on very clear outcomes.

Cognitive behavioral therapy is frequently best suited for individuals who are more relaxed with a structured and centered approach where the therapist also plays an educational role, in contrast to psychoanalytic forms of psychotherapy that encourage more open-ended self-exploration.

However, for CBT to be effective, the patient must be ready and willing to put in the time and effort necessary to analyze their ideas and feelings. Although self-analysis and study can be intimidating, understanding how personal states influence behavior outside of oneself is a terrific way to get started.

The short-term treatment of some types of emotional discomfort without the normal need for psychotropic drugs is also a good fit for cognitive behavioral therapy.

The ability to establish coping mechanisms that are useful both now and in the future is one of cognitive behavioral therapy's biggest advantages.

Actions in CBT

These steps are frequently included in CBT:

Recognize uncomfortable circumstances or living conditions. A mental health issue, divorce, sadness, rage, or other factors may be among them. You might have a lengthy conversation with your psychiatrist about the issues and objectives you wish to focus on.

Be aware of your thoughts, feelings, and beliefs around these matters. The psychiatrist will let you express your ideas once you've determined the problems that need to be addressed. Self-talk, the interpretation of the significance of a circumstance, and your perceptions of yourself, other people, and events can all be included in this. Your psychiatrist could advise you to write your thoughts down in a journal.

Recognize fuzzy or unfavorable thoughts. To assist you to comprehend the patterns of thought and behaviors that may have led to your query, the psychiatrist may urge you to pay close attention to how your body, mind, and behavior react in various situations.

Reframe the negative or vague concept. The psychologist would probably advise you to consider if your perception of a circumstance is grounded in reality or represents a distorted view of what is occurring. The transfer may be difficult. You might have ingrained beliefs about who you are and how to live. With practice, beneficial thought and behavior patterns will become automatic and won't require as much effort.

Neuroplasticity: what is it?

Neuroplasticity is the term used to describe the brain's propensity to rearrange itself during life by creating new neural connections. The brain's nerves (nerve cells) can modify their behavior to new circumstances or changes in their environment because of neuroplasticity, which also enables them to prepare for injury and sickness.

The brain can be reorganized through processes like "axonal sprouting," in which unharmed axons develop new nerve ends to replace neurons whose connections have been compromised. Additionally, unharmed axons will develop nerve endings, connect to other unharmed nerve cells, and form new brain pathways to carry out a required function.

For instance, if a brain hemisphere is damaged, some of its tasks may replace those of the hemisphere that is still intact. The brain also makes up for damage by rearranging and creating new connections between healthy neurons. Movement is necessary for the neurons to reconnect.

Neuroplasticity frequently causes impairment. For instance, sound-hungry brain cells can rewire in deaf people's ears, causing tinnitus, a persistent ringing sensation.

The nerves must be adequately stimulated for them to create helpful associations. Brain plasticity and malevolent brain plasticity are other names for neuroplasticity. Our thoughts continue to change as we learn more. Most of us behave and think substantially differently today than we did 20 years ago. Neuroplasticity is the term for the change that occurs as a result of our ability to observe, learn, and adapt.

Every time we think or feel something again, we build a brain pathway, and every time we think something new, we start to develop a new way of being. When such small changes occur frequently, our brains begin to modify the way they function.

The "muscle-forming" component of the brain is called neuroplasticity; we improve at the things we do frequently, and we lose interest in the things we don't. This is the physiological explanation for why engaging in a concept or practice repeatedly makes it stronger. Over time, it's becoming second nature to us. Essentially, we are what we say and do.

Lifelong neuroplasticity is ongoing. Depending on what is used, connections within the brain either get stronger or weaker. Younger people's brains are incredibly fluid, and they change quickly. As we become older, things change less naturally; the brain loses part of its elasticity, and our memories, understandings, and experiences become more fixed.

We will transform all we do and say by utilizing neuroplasticity because the brain is crucial to everything we do and say. To help you regain mental control, neuro feedback uses those straightforward neuroplasticity concepts.

The Neuroplasticity Theory and the Basic Principles

First, we must keep in mind that, even though we have provided a very concise explanation of neuroplasticity above, the reality is a little less clear. Neuroplasticity experts Christopher A. Shaw and Jill C. McEachern provide the following explanation: According to Shaw and McEachern, there are two main perspectives on neuroplasticity:

One of the fundamental mechanisms for any change in final brain activity or behavioral response is neuroplasticity.

The term "neuroplasticity" refers to a diverse range of abnormal brain adaptations and changes. The first perspective assumes that research on the subject will result in a full, all-inclusive neuroplasticity paradigm and is best suited for a single neuroplasticity hypothesis with some fundamental principles. For each behavior to be understood from the second viewpoint, many structures and processes will be required.

Sadly, I am unable to present a concise explanation of a unified neuroplasticity hypothesis here. All I can say with certainty is that this discipline is still in its infancy and that fresh discoveries are being made every day. We currently know that there are two primary categories of neuroplasticity:

Structural neuroplasticity, which refers to variations in the frequency of the neural (or neural) linkages.

Functional neuroplasticity, which explains how learning and development lead to long-lasting synaptic alterations.

We do know that some tasks can be re-routed, relearned, and re-established in the brain, but many of the exciting possibilities occur in changes to the internal structure of the brain. While all types of neuroplasticity hold fascinating promise, neural neuroplasticity is undoubtedly the one that is currently receiving the most attention.

Psychology and Neuroplasticity

These novel study directions are fascinating to biologists, chemists, and neuroscientists, but they are also fascinating to psychologists. Along with changes in the way the brain functions and adaptive adaptations, neuroplasticity may also offer opportunities for social advancement.

One may hypothesize, as Christopher Bergland puts it: "This cycle opens up the prospect of recreating oneself and moving away from the status quo or addressing prior traumatic events that produce anxiety and tension." Hardwired fear-based experiences can also help you develop habits of resistance that can keep you from living life to the fullest.

We already use pharmaceuticals and other medications to alter how our brains function and neuroscience has made great strides in learning how to alter how our brains function by altering the way we think. And if the simple acts we frequently perform during a typical day can permanently alter our brain's structure and function?

Learnability and Neuroplasticity

It is easy to understand how learning and neuroplasticity are related since when we think, new brain pathways are created. Every new experience has the potential to form new neuronal connections and change our brain's default mode of operation.

For instance, not all research is created equal—learning new information may not always benefit from the brain's incredible neuroplasticity, but learning a new language or musical instrument does. We might be able to learn how to purposefully restructure the brain through this kind of research.

The extent to which we enhance neuroplasticity and how we approach life, in general, will also determine how far we can push the brain's seemingly magical capabilities.

Children's Neuroplasticity

Children's brains are continually changing, growing, and evolving. With each new understanding, the structure, function, or both of the brains are improved. Each neuron in a child's brain has around 7,500 connections to other neurons at birth; by age 2, the neurons in the brain have more than twice as many connections as those in the brains of typical adults. These connections progressively go away as the child gets older and begin to form their distinct patterns and interactions.

Infants exhibit four different types of neuroplasticity:
Adaptive: changes that occur as young people practice a particular skill and allow the brain to adjust to functional or physiological changes in the brain (such as injuries).

Impairment: alterations brought on by hereditary or acquired disorders reorganization of existing, dysfunctional systems that is excessive and may result in dysfunction or diseases; these processes are quicker and more apparent in young children, allowing them to recover from wounds far faster than most adults. Infants exhibit extensive neuroplastic growth, recovery, and adaption.

Adult Neuroplasticity
Although it is not absent in adults, this ability is typically found at lower levels and in smaller amounts than in children. Despite this, the adult brain is still capable of remarkable improvement. It can increase memory, restore lost connections and capabilities that haven't been used in a while, and even enhance cognitive abilities all around. Although the ability is typically not as high in older adults as it is in children and young adults, both older people and younger people can foster positive change and development in their minds with consistent effort and a healthy lifestyle.

The advantages of neuroplasticity for the brain

According to the study we just discussed, the brain benefits from neuroplasticity in a variety of ways. These are some more ways your brain gains from brain adaptation in addition to the enhancements and advantages described above:

The ability to rewire brain functions (for example, if the region controlling one stimulus becomes affected, certain regions may be able to pick up the slack);

The loss of function in one area can improve senses in other areas (for example, if one sense is missing, the others will increase);

- Improved memory capacity;
- Improved cognitive abilities;
- Improved learning efficacies;

How Neuroplasticity Can Rewire Your Brain

Let's first comprehend some of the applications of neuroplasticity. The following techniques have been demonstrated to increase or induce neuroplasticity:

Intermittent fasting: (as previously mentioned) improves synaptic tolerance, promotes brain development, boosts general cognitive performance, and lowers the risk of neurodegenerative diseases;

Traveling: opens up new neural pathways and increases brain activity by exposing the brain to novel stimuli and surroundings;

Use mnemonics: strengthening prefrontal parietal connection through recall preparation;

Learning a musical instrument: helps create new neural networks and strengthen connections between different brain regions;

Exercises with the non-dominant hand can strengthen neuronal connectivity and create new brain connections;

Fiction reading strengthens and increases brain connectivity;

Increase your vocabulary, which helps with information processing and visual and aural functions;

Produce artwork: enhances "Default Mode Network" (or DMN) connectivity in the brain while it is at rest, which can enhance focus, concentration, memory, empathy, and introspection;

Sleeping: enhances memory recall by encouraging the creation of dendritic spines, which serve as neuronal connections and help convey information between cells;

Dancing: lowers the risk of Alzheimer's disease and improves brain connectivity.

Chapter Two

GRAB AND MAINTAIN ATTENTION

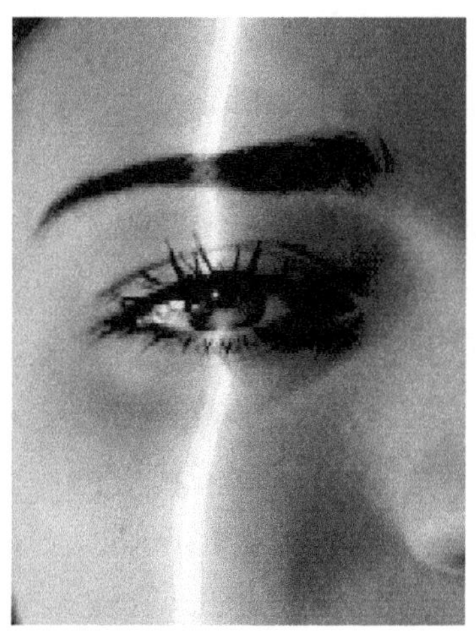

Gaining your conversation partner's attention is crucial before attempting to understand their thoughts. It's imperative to gain access to the other party first, and even more so, you must maintain that connection. The worst kind of distracted conversational companion is one who looks away. On the other hand, when your attention is divided, you foster a close bond between two people. First impressions matter, or how our beliefs affect our behavior.

Everyone has previously seen it: You quickly categorize someone you just met when you meet them for the first time. We can decide if we find someone empathetic or offensive in the first three to four seconds. However, not only we but also our rivals quickly determine whether we are reliable or not. There is tragically no second chance to make a good first impression because you are immediately placed in a box. To have a positive impact during those first few seconds, it is crucial to project seriousness, reliability, and security. Making it obvious which body signals must be sent out for us to form a favorable opinion of the discussion partner is another suggestion.

The problem is that because the language of the body is so fluid and made up of so many tiny individual muscle movements, we are unable to actively control it. A real smile has much more muscles engaged than a phony one, so you can tell the difference between the two right away. One would need to actively send a variety of appropriate signals in a split second to purposefully manage the first impression. That's quite unlikely. The presence does not seem real or behave as one would expect, and one would lose empathy and trust if even one signal is missing or not fully in sync with the others.

The speaker quickly gets the impression that something is off. Your thoughts, in contrast, provide a more effective means of influencing our charisma. Because our bodies automatically express everything we think without even realizing it. Even good thoughts tend to lead to a good attitude toward other people and a good charisma.

The language that people use and how they talk is fundamentally influenced by their environment. Thoughts have an impact on body language and facial emotions in particular. This makes sure that the other person's opinions are crucial to how you present yourself to them. Because all you feel or are driven by emotionally is transferred in a circumstance or a single position to your discussion partner. When a person is psychologically imprisoned in a particular setting, their body naturally falls back into simplistic thought patterns and action patterns.

When you feel a strong sense of grief and envision something tragic, you cannot jump for joy because of your emotional state. The contrary is also true: when we experience tremendous, joyful pleasure, we become melancholy and unable to let our shoulders drop and slide into the armchair. Therefore, you can only influence your charisma if you can also manage your emotions. The basic mind controls both the body and the emotions.

Additionally, changes in facial expressions and body language become more pronounced the more intensely an emotion is focused in one direction. The majority of people undoubtedly go through this every day in a variety of circumstances, whether consciously or unconsciously. For instance, when the tax office sends you letters, you may become upset because you have to pay taxes again. Soon after, you meet with a business partner and immediately feel the same way during the talk.

The unpleasant news from the tax office adds to unfavorable ideas, which only serve as a roadblock to the conversation. Since those negative ideas are exactly what our words and actions reflect. We certainly don't need to experience a bad circumstance like the one with the tax return payment. The ensuing stimulus must be activated by just thinking about it because one of our most powerful abilities is imagination. We can only create and sustain life through our thoughts, which include sounds, tastes, smells, and, most importantly, feelings. Because our subconscious mind is so strong, it cannot distinguish between fiction and reality, thus the concepts are true.

To use this communication tool, it is first necessary to address the following query: What is appropriate in a conversation? Because for the majority of people, that is where the issue is. Many people just don't want to, even though they don't know what they want. Whether you believe, "I don't want my interlocutor to be dissatisfied and upset," or "I want my interlocutor to be happy," does make a difference. If the aim is known, you can carefully assess which straightforward setting is most conducive to achieving it.

It is possible to train oneself to have an optimistic outlook on life. This calls for a previously established trigger. The thumb and index finger, or something similar, can be used for this. The second stage is to search for a constructive idea or connection that might be useful when speaking to someone. The objective of these first two steps is to picture the relevant circumstance. The best method to do that is to close your eyes since it improves focus. You will be able to perceive sights, sounds, and feelings more readily the more vividly you can picture the scene. It's crucial to push your own sensory experience if you want to comprehend even the smallest nuances. If the condition is sensed spiritually, the images, sounds, and feelings can be enhanced and grounded with the stimuli. It stores the fundamentally upbeat structure in the brain and may be accessed at any time by pressing a button, increasing one's charisma as a result. The initial steps to contact:

Openness

A welcoming body language conveys this to the other person. In contrast, crossed arms act as a kind of exclusionary shield. The same holds if you have your hands in your pockets. Being open demonstrates a certain level of self-assurance and increases charisma. However, the same holds here as well: being or playing open-mindedly is useless.

The posture will automatically open if you identified the proper default option in the previous step and disabled it now. Transparent body language includes gestures like raising the palms of the hands or taking a tiny step in the direction of the person you are speaking with.

Keeping a gaze

The majority of individuals avoid it and find it awkward to look someone in the eyes. We can tell we are paying attention to our conversation partner when we look into his eyes. The optimum place to look between the eyes is at the base of the nose since both eyes cannot be seen at once. Additionally, you can attempt to ascertain the other person's eye color. It compels you to make eye contact and to look someone in the eye. We allow our counterparts to perceive our basic emotions through the eyes, along with our moods and thoughts.

The other individual perceives a challenge and will respond. You'll come out as either uninterested or shy if you don't return the other guy's attention. Being the first to strike the head is important. That exhibits an attempt. It hurts more the longer you maintain eye contact. It almost seems unnecessary to state: It is thought to be weird to be searching for a long time.

By the way, you can also tell if someone is involved by looking at the students. The dilated pupils are a real indication of approval. Pupil dilating can occur for a variety of causes, including inadequate lighting or an irritated person. When the interlocutor's pupil starts to enlarge, you can assume that he is deeply engaged. It is impossible to stop the instinctive mechanism that causes pupil dilation.

Greeting

For business visits and other formal occasions, handshakes are the customary greeting. The other person's hand shouldn't be broken, he shouldn't feel like he's reaching for a dead fish, and the tone should be kind. Shaking hands should be done with respect and power. The majority of folks salute in anticipation of this. The person participating in the encounter instinctively understands something is wrong if it goes differently than intended. It's crucial to pay attention to the other person's name if multiple people are being invited at once.

Remembering to repeat the name a few times at the beginning of the lecture is the simplest approach to memorizing it. However, instead of saying "Mr. John, Mr. John, Mr. John," say "Hi Mr. I am excited to meet you. Mr. John, get seated. You ought to get a little closer so that you may emphasize the open body vocabulary once more. The interlocutor always sends signals at the first meeting. First of all, you truly get the first impression of his current situation.

You can't shake hands with everyone after speaking in front of a group. But you should make an effort to get along with everyone. It is plausible to think that you would connect each one with threads from your own life. By observing the people, you do this one at a time. However, you don't move forward in order; instead, you start at a certain position and repeatedly alter your route, moving first to the left behind, then to the right, then to the middle, etc. You extend the hypothetical lines in as many directions as you can.

The scenario can be comprehended best by observing the frequent changes in direction, which indicate that various individuals in the space question how they are being handled. Just be careful to preserve those threads. A new thread is automatically tensioned when a thread splits, meaning the relation and consequently, the focus ceases. Therefore, you already have a "nice line" for the crowd that will enchant them.

People Drawer

Charm translates to "bewitch" or "fascinate" in French. People with charisma are aware of their attraction to other men. Charm has a kind of magnetic pull that has a spell-like effect on other people. Natural charisma makes correspondence easier. Communication is considerably easier when a person is charming. But charming behavior can also be taught to it.

Outside manifestation

First, the appearance on the outside is discernible. Despite the notion that inner principles are infallible, we frequently allow external factors to influence us. Would you trust your bank advisor with your money if he showed up wearing a tattered shirt and scuffed jeans? What we wear affects how we perceive ourselves.

The halo effect is what it is referred to as in social psychology. That implies that a single favorable characteristic determines our total opinion of a person. The popularity of other apps is declining. Additionally, the person is automatically given several favorable traits that frequently connect to the dominant attribute. As a result, handsome or wealthy people are regarded as wiser than those who are less attractive or less wealthy.

Examining the interviews with David Rainey and Denise Mack also demonstrated how important outer appearance is in choosing an applicant. If they looked nice in their attire, hairstyle, makeup, and jewelry, they might have a better chance of getting an interview. The participants insisted on the contrary, but the professional training was sidelined. Our opponent doesn't even have to choose consciously.

These are messages we are sending subconsciously by way of our shoes. Everyone has goals they wish to see accomplished, but at the same time, everyone has certain dreams. So when we meet an expert, we assume the medical professional should be dressed in white, if not a white coat. It informs us that the man is a doctor and that we may entrust him with our medical issues. The doctor's outfit serves as a kind of label identifying him and his specialties. By clothing in the manner in which you want to be recognized, you will benefit from this choice of marking.

In any circumstance, having access to expert contacts is essential. It never hurts to be aware of your perceived strengths and flaws and to emphasize or conceal them as necessary. A well-tailored suit or the appropriate hairdo for men can be successful, as can subtle lipstick, form-fitting gowns, and high heels for women. However, if you highlight the wrong traits, you could come across as foolish.

Additionally, a strong fragrance is required because smells have an unconscious impact on us. The usage of perfume should be so subtle that it is barely perceptible. Your image will also be communicated through both large and tiny things. One is that purchasing a high-end vehicle will elevate one's status. (No one should be aware that it is a rental car.) In the end, it comes down to how the other person is feeling. Relationships tend to take longer to develop when he is attracted to fancy cars for some reason.

Yes, you should probably do some research before taking the fancy car to the meeting. For stores that are closed in traditional sectors where there is a lot of money, accessories like the ideal jacket, a stylish watch, and the just-stated luxury car are unquestionably an advantage. It's important to keep in mind where the conversation is taking place. If it is your workplace, you should design the layout yourself. The other party can be significantly influenced by the right room decor, awards, and subtle but impactful wall decorations. The customer will continue with greater maturity and improved abilities, which is fantastic for communication.

Personality perception

Both the outer appearance and the personality are important for the first impression. Self-confidence is crucial in this situation. It's essential to comprehend their advantages. It offers protection for communications with other people. Self-confidence is a mental construct that has nothing to do with how others perceive you. You should develop your skills further once you are aware of them and know how to apply them. If you list all of your best traits on paper and read them aloud to yourself every morning, you'll become even more self-aware. It builds self-confidence without being impolite. By taking a modest dose of bravery, you will feel more confident. Most people struggle to interact with others or communicate at events. It entails training and surmounting so that the performances don't appear rehearsed or hazardous.

After a while, it becomes simpler, and you continue to be confident and at ease even in challenging and uncomfortable circumstances. You must be confident in your actions as a prerequisite for this. People who experience particularly severe concerns and obstructions when they need to communicate with others, for instance, can approach the issue cautiously.

For the time being, ask those who are walking along the street. It doesn't matter what occurs because it isn't about anything. As a result, you get more comfortable meeting new people and the threshold for resistance is lowered. When you are enthusiastic about something, you can only inspire others to do the same. People who are self-assured and express their opinions on their work. They aren't debating it; instead, they are getting right to the point.

You won't find your equivalent entry if you are configured for your benefit. As a result, you need to put a lot of effort into your comparison. This quality is crucial for making friends and persuading others to agree with your viewpoints. Because you can only imagine yourself this way in other people's thoughts.

People who are kind, compassionate, encouraging, enthusiastic, truthful, and warm-hearted treat others differently than those who lack these qualities or who believe that they are not in demand in the workplace. The tone of voice, body language, and facial expressions must all match the uttered words to appear trustworthy to others and foster faith. Congruence is the term for agreement. When the body language is inconsistent with the tone and meaning of what is being stated, the interlocutor can usually tell. If it already occurs, this will make contact or split impossibly.

It just doesn't work when someone attempts to speak in a joyful tone while lowering his head and displaying a dejected countenance. Because the spoken word and the body language do not always convey the same meaning, you can see that something is off right away.

Making deals with friends

"Like and loves to join" and "Opposites attract" are two proverbs that are equally well-known and widely used in everyday speech. Is one true and the other false, or do they both contain some truth? Everyone has probably had the pleasure of meeting someone and feeling at ease in their presence right away. One felt at ease and understood. This frequently occurs when you immediately express an opinion, share a profession or interest, or both during a chat. Perhaps it was also a subconscious similarity in speech patterns, breathing patterns, or mood. Whatever the case, it was a shared experience that allowed you and this person to interact on the same level and establish a confidant relationship.

Thus, the adage "like and likes to join" is entirely accurate. Ask yourself this question: Who attracts you? Are these individuals seeking exactly the opposite of what you have in mind? People, that hold radically divergent opinions from your own? Do you ever think to yourself, "Nice that you disagree with me,"?

Not. Because people who resemble one another often get along. View your friends' groups from different angles. Most likely, you don't consciously consider it. You will discover, however, that your hobbies, values, and way of life are similar to those of your friends upon deeper examination. However, there is some validity to the adage "opposites attract."

A slight variation between two extremely similar persons can create a certain attraction and be very pleasant. Consider "Dick und Goof" as an example of a television show or film that frequently features antagonistic characters. The two characters are utterly dissimilar to one another. The stories are only compelling and worth witnessing when opposites create friction points. It is possible to consistently see this occurrence in both professional and ordinary settings. For instance, if you want to purchase a car, you will be more inclined to do so from a likable car dealer than from one who lacks charm. But if it's intrusive it will have a detrimental effect on the decision to buy because it is uncomfortable.

Numerous variables affect whether a buyer finds a salesperson to be pleasant or uncomfortable. When you notice similarities, even if they are limited to speech patterns, you usually find him to be likable. For instance, we will have faith in a merchant if he resembles a friend or a good buddy.

According to an examination of insurance recommendations, people are more likely to get insurance from a salesperson who shares their values. We typically share a lot of things with our friends, which is precisely why we feel empathy and trust. We speak the same language and use the same phrases, so we could go on and on about future car purchases. If the connection is good enough, we won't need to say much. Therefore, it's critical to find common ground with your conversation partner. For instance, this entails changing how you speak. If the other person speaks calmly and methodically, you can easily establish a common ground for conversation if you do the same.

Establish a common basis

This tactic is quite useful since it allows us to explore the territory of second-person thinking. This urges us to show support for and have the same thoughts as our coworkers. This will make it easier for us to understand where we are and how to proceed.

You can not only look for common ground but also create it. Consciously imitating the body language and psychology of the other person is the best strategy for achieving consensus. We are letting our listeners know that we are getting near in that regard.

You react to the other person's actions after seeing their conduct. Hypnotherapist and industry pioneer Milton H. Erickson almost adopted this strategy. He mimicked his counterpart, which allowed him to quickly establish a person's trust even though he had never met him before.

He has focused particularly on nonverbal cues from the body. Why? What we say is crucial, but so is how we say it and convey it with our body language and facial emotions. Different interpretations of the spoken words will result from differences in voice and body language. The actors need to practice saying "no" in various contexts. A very good illustration of this is the Dr. Fox experiment, carried out in the USA in 1970.

A presentation was given before a group of psychiatrists, psychologists, and teachers by an actress who identified herself as a specialist in the application of mathematics to human behavior. Although the text was complete rubbish, nobody noticed. The purported specialist persuaded and conveyed what was said in the manner he did through his words. The Dr. Fox experiment demonstrates the significant impact of speech and body language on communication in this way.

What does this entail in terms of establishing a standard for company conduct? Let's choose z. An overview workshop for the staff. The boss should respond more subtly and adjust if he believes the employee is acting calmer than he is. He may frequently mimic his sitting stance.

Through these comparisons, he gains confidence and accomplishes his goal more quickly. For instance, it also works the other way around. There are countless details to display. Scientific research supports: Different postures, attitudes, and gestures imply that you are speaking the same language. For instance, it has been demonstrated that waitresses who matched their customers received greater tips than those who did not. Tanya L. Chartrand and John A. Bargh discovered in another study that similarities can have a positive impact on people's compassion values.

The participants conversed with an additional individual who had been introduced. Others were repeated by the interlocutor, while others weren't. The outsider was more endearing to those who had been copied than the others.

You should just adopt a few of the other person's characteristics to acquire a sense of them to find common ground. It avoids exaggeration. It seems unnatural when you urgently try to carry out every task in the same manner as you're comparable. For one to feel gradually toward the other, it must function harmoniously. In essence, one should want this cycle to occur naturally. The only way to expose real individuals is in that way.

Position and motion

Some various gestures and attitudes can be mimicked. You should respond to the following inquiries to be aware of these choices:

- How do I stand in general?
- What's the expression on my face?
- Am I hunching over?
- Which way should I turn my head?
- Where are my shoulders located?
- The best way to hold my arms
- What grip should I use?
- My torso is inclined?
- How do I shift my upper body in that direction?
- How are my legs positioned?
- How close together are my feet?
- Which motions stand out?

The better you know yourself, the more accurately you can mimic your counterpart's conduct.

Voicing and expression

Another quick and efficient method of establishing rapport is by mirroring the words and expressions. Since there may not be much-shared body language during phone calls, it works particularly effectively. You should pay great attention to what the other person says. Here, many attributes are repeatable.

The timbre establishes the pitch of a sound. You're elevating yourself a little bit if you're now speaking to someone with a fairly high voice. But: Don't go overboard. Nobody should think you're mocking him. The link would then lose its strength, making a new one impossible. Because of this, the depth and breadth of the expression for each particular word may only be somewhat increased.

Our vocabulary is unusual because of its speed. Some folks speak so quickly that it's difficult to hear them. On the other side, there are those men whose sentences we finish in our heads or even out loud because they speak too slowly. The size is familiar to the speakers. You must be mindful to speak in brief phrases when engaging in this conduct right now. So there is no possibility of getting lost. If you wish to mimic a slower speech rate, simply take short pauses in between each sentence.

This communicates to the opposing side how long it will take. In general, you should be aware of where the other person takes breaks. You can carry it out for yourself if you notice a pattern here. It will come effortlessly for you to get an understanding of the other person's speech pattern when you focus on the breaks. Is the tone of the sentence consistently even and nearly monotone, or does it fluctuate depending on the words or locations? You might be able to recall and adopt a tune.

Another significant aspect of language is represented by the volume. You should also adjust to the other party, but not too much. A loud voice, incidentally, doesn't always indicate that the other person has a hearing impairment. Additionally, a weak voice need not be an indication of timidity or lack of confidence.

You should take note of similar words when you are aware that the other person does so. People frequently use words and expressions that are unique to their context, profession, or pastime. It's best if the pastime can be turned into a topic of conversation for work: You might state "Now only square is the oval" in place of "you still have to sign here." Speaking the other person's language is ultimately what matters.

Some persons can speak in a variety of accents and dialects while yet sounding genuine. That really should be a must. If not, the other person may very easily feel deceived or even insulted. Especially if he would not want his vocabulary or accent to be heard.

Breathing our level of sensation is closely related to how we breathe. To begin with, when we are aroused, we breathe very quickly and shallowly; on the other hand, when we are relaxed, we breathe slowly and gently. Watching his chest rise and fall is the best approach to mimic the other person's breathing. Gestures made with the shoulders and the diaphragm can also hint at the pattern. You'll be surprised at how potent the pattern is if you follow it.

Moods

The discussion partner's moods can be mirrored in the moods. We judge people's likeability based on the mentality they are in at the time. For instance, it's not very useful to react to your counterpart's gloomy mood with intense happiness. It's best to make an effort to notice this emotional state and get a sense of how you're feeling. The interlocutor can also be led into a more optimistic basic mood if he feels like he is being heard.

When you observe that your conversation partner is joyful, you will also catch this feeling and feed it. He will experience our wonderful energy, which will make him feel much better. Opinions In a dispute, divergent viewpoints frequently clash. Nevertheless, to establish a strong connection with the other party, we must respect his opinions. Who, after all, wants to be with those who contest or criticize their beliefs? Of course, you are under no obligation to agree with your opponent's viewpoint. However, you do agree with a little portion of your case. You don't have to lie to demonstrate approval if you're going to take this issue up and think about it.

Lead the charge

The previous section covered a variety of tactics for creating consensus through copying other people's activities. Once you master this method, you can employ it without difficulty or concern. You are consequently exposed to outsiders right away. The portal to the world filled with mirror images of its counterpart is now open.

Giacomo Rizzolatti, an Italian neurophysiologist, and his team at the University of Parma discovered in the middle of the 1990s that macaque monkeys replicated humans' grabbing motions for food fairly instantly. The device that imitated human behavior. The Rizzolatti or mirror neurons that are in charge of this are the nerve cells.

Later, it was shown that the human brain is likewise susceptible to this disorder. Our brain can map and transmit whatever is felt through the sensory pathways because of mirror neurons. The other person's emotions and motor actions are both represented concurrently by the subconscious. Hello, z. B. A human can become infected very rapidly, and yawn.

However, the mirror neurons' activities are also triggered by all other visual, auditory, tactile, olfactory, smelt, and gustatory stimuli. This basic natural approach creates a connection with the other person, which functions better independently of how well you suit the other person. Additionally, the greater the number of matches, the quicker our actions can mimic their opposite. It makes it easier to exert control over other people's ideas and behaviors.

Therefore, if you gradually duplicate the characteristics of the other person, whether consciously or unconsciously, you will eventually reach a stage where you may take things a step further and begin making changes. When you reach this stage, you are aware that you and your counterpart have reached a considerable deal of agreement.

Internal perception

Understanding how our colleague absorbs and interprets information will help us respond to them more effectively. Our five senses help us experience the world around us. They prefer meaning-related human sensory sources. Therefore, you can begin to envision what you've seen mostly in the photos if someone questions us about anything. However, it is equally conceivable that you either think or feel that you are experiencing the sounds.

The three most significant processes by which we transfer information to experience are thinking, hearing, and sensing. There are also tastes and smells, which we will disregard in the following because they come second to interacting with other people. Simply said, everyone makes use of all sensory pathways.

Everyone prefers a particular way of perception, even though neither the visual nor the aural sense systems are exclusively used by each individual. Although the visual media often physically inspires us, our subconscious minds may also be influenced by sounds and emotions. If we can now identify which sensory system our conversation partner prefers, we will be able to adapt to it. The other person will understand and interpret our information more clearly.

Visual learners

People who have a strong visual sensory channel tend to speak and think in images. They either have a significant impact on colors and shapes or they are more conscious of them. They create visual concepts. The individual images in the head move very quickly about one another. They do this because speaking more quickly than others causes their voice to seem a little nasal and higher. Most of the time, visual individuals breathe from their chest. Their actions and verbal choices in particular make them easy to identify.

They frequently make gestures with their hands and fingers and utilize words like:

- Depict
- Check out
- View and observe
- Consider
- Detect
- Focus
- Illustrate
- Clarity
- Visible Sharpness
- See
- Cloudy
- Overview
- Imagine Idea
- Demonstrat

This list might be increased. If you pay close attention to what the other person is saying, you can easily determine whether they prefer the visual sensory system. The following are some common phrases:

- That is something I can imagine.
- I can imagine that I still don't understand it.
- That makes sense to me.
- I feel like it's a little hazy.
- I'm trying to get a sense of it.
- In my judgment, it appears that
- I can visualize it in my head.
- It is evident that I momentarily noticed a light.
- My perspective is different.
- Could I take a peek?

Auditory individuals

Audience-focused individuals talk in spoken words and sentences, which they can also hear as inner voices. These skills are particularly adept at listening and perceptive of background noise and human speech. He uses a lot of words and is very conscious of how he uses them and what he emphasizes. To him, it matters how something is said. He is therefore traveling steadily and gently. His breathing is calm and steady, and it makes his voice sound clear and whole. Crossed arms and folded hands are outward indicators of a recognized person. He seems to tilt his head slightly to the side and directs his ear at the other person speaking. It demonstrates that he pays attention.

Typical words heard include:
- Hinted
- Argue
- To talk about Talk Tell Whisper
- Hearing
- Listen Sound Listen Chatter Talk Say Speak Voice
- Deaf
- Volume Suggest

Of course, the list itself is completely flexible. One can speak effectively to an audience while using words like these. Those who are auditory-minded frequently use the idioms listed below:
- That seems reasonable.
- Identical words.
- That is a good idea.
- What is it about?
- Never heard of it before.
- I'll voice my opinion.
- They extol its benefits.
- He informed her of the news.
- Give me a listen.
- The engine makes a cat-like purr.
- Truth be told...
- Tell me about... The music is created by sound.
- You won't get anywhere with me.
- Let's set the tone for the day.

Kinesthetic individuals

People with a strong propensity for kinesthetic can be found in their emotions. To remember, look for the emotion that contributed to the specific condition. The kinesthetic form tries to touch things to feel what they feel and how they look. His behavior and word choice are based on these emotional experiences. Along with his emotions, he pays close attention to gestures. He typically uses all of his body when interacting. Compared to the visual and auditory folks, it takes a long time to gather the information you need, making talking even slower. The various words are separated by lengthy pauses.

The quiet, beautiful voice that results from deep abdominal breathing gives the kinesthetic person a generally serene appearance. The phrases listed below best describe him:

- Touch
- Take care of
- gut reaction
- Empathize
- Freezing
- Feel Experience
- Comprehensible
- Hold firmly
- Palpable
- Palpable
- Hard Comprehend
- Gently
- Shock

- Feel Motionless
- Joining forces

Typical language for kinesthetic individuals is:
- We'll control that, I promise.
- I have no idea why that is.
- Very cold.
- My intuition tells me
- We must lay all of our cards on the table.
- Such alarmist rhetoric.
- I have to acknowledge that.
- I get a headache from it.
- They flipped everything on its head.
- We communicate.
- I can adhere to you.
- Let's move cautiously.
- I'm eager.
- That returns to being straight.
- I feel optimistic about

You'll be able to reply to him and comprehend his language even better if you pay attention to which of the three senses the person you're speaking to is using. You must pay close attention while you define and listen.

Imagine, for instance, that a visual form and kinesthetics collide. Most likely, the image would make it difficult for his opponent to picture it. He can, however, plainly illustrate this by making a lot of quick movements quickly. He can also ponder whether the individual to whom he is referring sees something identical to himself or whether he still has some doubts.

However, since the kinesthetic form's inner perception is different, it will now have severe difficulty following at all. The counterpart will be able to comprehend what you are trying to say to him more clearly if the picture adjusts to the kinesthetic form by speaking more slowly, pausing more frequently, and using appropriate phrases and idioms.

You will first make an effort to communicate with your discussion partner across all three networks if it is not immediately clear which kind of sensations they prefer. Most of the time, you can tell right away which one he is responding to the eyes can inform us. In essence, the stories are dissimilar.

Each word, however, focuses on just one of the three main sensory pathways. There is information on the Eiffel Tower in one narrative. The second one is about turning on the radio and playing your favorite music. The third describes an experience and the emotions that went along with it. Simply asking someone to recall what they have read and seen through their eyes will reveal what story the viewer was picturing. These provide evidence of the viewer's perceptions.

With visual perceptions, the eyes travel in the higher region. The other person's gaze travels upward toward the viewer if they recall what they saw. However, as you begin to create images, your eyes begin to shift to the left and upward. The other person is watching a game indoors if they are staring into space or pointing straight ahead. When they picture it, some people also choose to ignore it.

The sense is auditory if the eyes move in the center. The other person hears sounds and noises from their memories when they move their eyes to the right. Left-facing eyes indicate that sounds and noises are created inwardly. When you talk to yourself, the eyes behave differently. Then the eyes go to the right, downward. Feelings come into play if the eyes cast a glance down to the left. Such a view implies that emotions are evoked and triggered. These involuntarily occurring eye movements are typically only seen for a brief period.

This summary aids in understanding how the other person sees things. The access information is inverted for some people. It's simple to learn, for instance, by asking for a visual cue, like the color of your car. The access information is likely inverted if you look to the upper left.
Why is it even important to have this information? Knowing how to reach your opponent through which medium or with which examples makes communication simpler. Thus, the agreement is attained. By doing so, you can roam around with your ideas while also seeing how your conversation partner is thinking.

It is possible to determine whether the other person can follow their instructions using the eye access information. For instance, if you ask him to envision something and he turns away, you need to switch up your approach to get his attention.

The ability to access information through the eyes also allows for direct communication of the conversation partner's thoughts. You can add, "You can probably envision that," if you notice, for instance, that he is looking up.

Chapter Three

THE POWER OF POSITIVE THINKING: EMOTIONAL INTELLIGENCE

Different definitions of emotional intelligence have been put out by scientists and psychologists over the years as they seek to comprehend why some people can be intelligent (academically brilliant) while being ignorant of human emotions and sentiments. The capacity to detect one's own emotions as well as those of others, to distinguish between various emotions, and categorize those emotions appropriately is known as emotional intelligence.

The ability to manage and/or alter emotions to adapt to settings or achieve one's goals depends on the ability to use emotional information to drive thinking and behavior. An emotionally intelligent person can be recognized because they exhibit the traits listed below:

- They are adept at resolving challenging circumstances amicably.

- They have a clear way of expressing their ideas and opinions.

- They win the admiration and respect of others.

- Their acts and thoughts have an impact on other individuals.

- They are adept at persuading others to lend a hand.

- Under pressure, they maintain their composure they are aware of how their emotional reactions would influence other people or circumstances.

- They are aware of when and how to say the "correct" thing to get the desired outcomes.

- They know how to motivate themselves and others to perform at their best when negotiating. They handle themselves and manage others successfully.

- Even in trying circumstances, they consistently have a positive attitude.

Our emotions are what motivate us to act in the manner that we do, and this can have a positive or negative impact on those around us. More often than not, than your intelligence, people will judge you based on how you respond to them. Being in control of your emotions is the key, and if you lack this power, changing how you behave is impossible. Psychologists once believed that you needed to fully express your undesirable or negative feelings to move past them. Cognitive behavior therapy is one of the methods that psychologists and schizophrenics have created to assist people to communicate their negative or unpleasant feelings.

It tends to keep you down to linger on your negative emotions. The hurt and unpleasant emotions might fade over time, but they would have left enough of a mark on you that you might start to react badly to those around you.

The Blocks of Emotional Intelligence That Form

Your emotional intelligence is derived from four fundamental components that function as DNA's building blocks. These components, which form the foundation of your emotional intelligence, enable you to acquire particular skills and abilities when nourished with experience. However, unlike your biological DNA, the building blocks of emotional intelligence may be improved, allowing you to significantly raise your emotional intelligence. The groundbreaking psychologist's John Mayer of the University of New Hampshire and Peter Salovey of Yale, who jointly invented the phrase emotional intelligence in 1990, identified these four building elements.

Each piece of the puzzle stands for a set of skills that collectively form your emotional intelligence. Each level incorporates and builds on the talents of the levels below it in a hierarchical structure. The four foundational elements are:

- The capacity to recognize, evaluate, and express emotion with accuracy.
- The capacity to produce or access feelings on command when doing so will help you better comprehend yourself or another else.
- The capacity to comprehend emotions and the information they produce.

- The capacity to control one's emotions to foster both emotional and intellectual development.

Emotional Intelligence Categories

There are five main categories of talents connected with emotional intelligence, according to psychologists. Understanding your emotions and how they affect your ideas and conduct is known as self-awareness. Understanding your strengths, weaknesses, and self-confidence comes from self-awareness.

Self-regulation is the capacity to control your impulsive actions and emotions. Although it doesn't prevent you from experiencing feelings, emotional intelligence gives you the ability to judge how long a feeling should stay. The ability to control your emotions, adjust to change, and keep your word are all crucial components of self-regulation.

There are a variety of techniques you can use to control your negative emotions, such as meditation and viewing problems from a more optimistic perspective.

You need the following qualities to be able to self-regulate:

- Self-control
- Trustworthiness
- Conscientiousness
- Adaptability
- Innovation

The inner force that pushes you toward a goal is called motivation. You must establish clear objectives, specify a course of action, and maintain a positive outlook at all times. Everyone has an attitude, whether it's positive or negative, at all times. However, with the right motivation, you can train your mind to focus more on a positive attitude. To reach your goals, you may turn any negative mindset into a good one.

You need to possess the following traits to be motivated:
- Attainment motivation
- Commitment Initiative
- Optimism

Empathy is the capacity to comprehend another person's feelings, worries, and wants. Understanding group dynamics and emotional cues can help you respond and react constructively to other people's emotions. Empathy can help you do this. Empathizers excel in helping others, serving others, utilizing diversity, and having political awareness. The capacity to cultivate interpersonal skills can help you succeed in both your job and personal life. The ability to comprehend, motivate, sympathize with, and successfully interact with people is a social skill that is necessary in today's tiny world.

Social abilities allow you to:
- Encourage others
- Interact with others
- form enduring connections
- Make money-making leads

Due to Its Smartness, Emotional Intelligence

EI is defined in slightly different ways by various persons. However, in general, it refers to the capacity to be aware of, cognizant of, and in control of one's own and other people's emotions. Similar to regular intelligence, this talent allows you to use emotional information to direct your thoughts and actions. It entails using knowledge in a way that advances your objectives. But when you have the kind of intelligence that schools test, you mostly work with words, figures, and facts.

You are utilizing your understanding of emotions when using EI. Some people simply have a natural ability to get along with others and comprehend their emotions. We often use phrases like "She's terrific with people" or "It almost seems like he can read my mind" when referring to these folks. Others appear to be particularly adept at identifying their goals and pursuing them. We use phrases like "She knows her own mind" or "Once he has his mind set on something, nothing is going to stop him" when referring to these people.

These are the types of individuals who have high EI. They perform well at home, school, and the office because of their capacity to comprehend and make use of emotional information. They are also natural leaders because of their capacity for self-expression and influence. Success in a variety of spheres of life seems to be correlated with EI.

The good news is that El appears to have learned most things. As you develop and gain knowledge from your experiences, it keeps expanding. This implies that with a little work, even if you aren't quite an emotional genius right now, you can become one. Why even try? El is useful in a variety of circumstances.

For instance: When you're upset, it might help you keep your cool. It can inspire you to pursue your objectives.

It can assist you in recognizing when someone is lying to you and in dealing with bullies and other challenging people. Perhaps most significantly, it may help you learn more about a pretty fascinating person: you!

Advantages of High Emotion Intelligence

An advantage over others and the ability to seize more opportunities come from having a high level of emotional intelligence. Numerous people have excellent academic credentials yet lead unhappy lives. This is due to their extreme incompetence when it comes to interpersonal connections. High emotional intelligence has a variety of advantages, including:

Personal effectiveness

To succeed in life, one must possess emotional intelligence. You are then better able to manage both your affairs and those of others. Your ability to control your emotions, whether they are positive or negative, depends on how emotionally intelligent you are. Emotional intelligence gives you tools to help you become more self-aware.

Thinking abilities

Even the most challenging circumstances can occasionally be overcome with ease if your perspective is changed. A high level of emotional intelligence will enable you to think strategically, which will motivate you and those around you. Professional connections to be able to relate to others well and work harmoniously with them, you must be able to comprehend how they think and behave.

Being emotionally intelligent helps you engage and communicate with people in productive ways.

Possessing leadership qualities

A good leader can relate to the people he is in charge of. With strong emotional intelligence, you'll be able to persuade, influence, inspire, and motivate others with ease. The ability to recognize and appropriately respond to other people's emotions is a leader's most attractive trait. This fosters a setting at work where more fruitful interactions can occur.

Physical fitness

Your level of general well-being will depend on your emotional intelligence. Your emotional state and stress levels are closely tied, and if you have high emotional intelligence, you'll be better able to deal with life's obstacles. Your physical abilities are weakened by high-stress levels and poor emotional intelligence, which lowers your immune system and lowers your quality of life.

Optimal mental health

How emotionally knowledgeable you are will greatly influence your attitude and perspective on life. Anxiety, despair, and mood swings are more likely to occur if your emotional intelligence is low. Your life will become dull and unpleasant as a result of this decreasing positivism and optimism. To accurately evaluate your emotions, you must be psychologically stable.

Conflict resolution

Conflict occurs frequently, and your capacity to resolve it greatly depends on your awareness of other people's feelings. The ability to comprehend and empathize with the feelings and viewpoints of others will make it simpler to resolve or avoid conflict. A high emotional intelligence level makes you a better negotiator since it helps you understand other people's needs and wants when resolving conflicts.

Success

The result of your internal drivers and self-assurance is your capacity for concentration on your goal. You are more self-disciplined to concentrate on reaching your objectives if you have a greater level of emotional intelligence. Additionally, you develop a stronger network of supporters, persevere with remarkable tenacity, and get past the obstacles standing in your way of achievement. By sacrificing short-term gains for long-term gains, emotional intelligence improves your chances of success.

Confidence Building

You'll feel more confident as you get to know yourself better. Faith in oneself and one's talents is confidence. As you become more conscious of your personality strengths, this will undoubtedly develop. Being confident need not translate into unnecessarily smug behavior. It simply means that you won't let irrational self-doubts hold you back. You won't feel helpless and despairing in the face of difficulty. Instead, you'll be motivated to apply your knowledge to meet the challenge.

The time has come to get to know yourself better. Start by posing the following queries to yourself: What are the main personality traits and skills I possess? Which five goals have they assisted me in achieving? What are my areas of weakness—the things I struggle with or have yet to learn? What are five things I can do to improve upon or compensate for these flaws? You can benefit from having this level of self-awareness in a variety of scenarios. Let's take the scenario where you wish to try out for the soccer squad. You haven't played soccer much in the past.

However, you are aware that you are the kind of person that will attend practices and give everything you have. You're skilled at cooperating with others. You're a quick runner and enjoy making new friends. Being aware of all the things working in your favor gives you the courage to try something new.

In the end, self-awareness educates you about other individuals in addition to oneself. Consider joining a soccer team but finding it difficult to get along with a teammate. Every practice you give it your all. Your teammate adopts a more relaxed attitude. You understand that there is no right or incorrect style because you are aware of the various personality types. Just you and your teammate. You can benefit from having this level of self-awareness in a variety of scenarios. Let's assume you're considering going out because you have a new perspective on life, which is a very positive thing.

You can both maintain your equilibrium by cooperating as a team. The more laid-back approach of your buddy helps you avoid being too hard on yourself. Your dedication keeps your teammate from taking a break.

Giving and receiving in this way benefit both parties. It is an essential component of any healthy partnership and the starting point of genuine human understanding.

How to Strengthen Self Control

Self-discipline is the ability to carry out your duties. Sometimes exercising self-control entails sacrificing your current convenience or pleasures for long-term success. To begin with, if you want to get physically fit, you might put up with the 5:00 a.m. gym torture to receive the long-term benefits of being secure and feeling terrific.

Recognize your weaknesses. Everybody is vulnerable. They do have similar effects on humans, whether they are foods like potato chips or chocolate chip cookies, apps like Twitter, or the newest addictive gaming gear. No matter what your shortcomings may be, acknowledge them. People strive to hide their defects or try to pretend they don't have them all too frequently. Recognize your shortcomings. You cannot overcome anything until you do.

Keep temptations away. Out of sight, out of mind, as they say. Although it may sound silly, this sentence offers sound guidance. Simply eliminating the biggest temptations from your life will greatly improve your self-control. If you want to eat better, avoid buying junk food. To increase your efficiency at work, mute your phone and disable notifications. You'll be more focused on reaching your objectives the fewer distractions there are in your environment. Remove negative influences to set yourself up for success.

Set specific objectives and create an action plan. You must have a distinct understanding of your goals if you want to develop self-discipline. You should also define what performance means to you. After all, if you don't know where you are heading, it's simple to get off track or lose your way. Every action you must take to accomplish your goals is laid out in a clear plan. Determine your identity and your activities. Make up a mantra to help you stay in the present. Successful people employ this tactic to maintain course and establish a distinct finish line.

Begin Small. You don't have to be a whole different person when you get up. On New Year's Day, as a custom, people frequently set resolutions in the hopes that this year would be different. Okay, you can update it this year, but you don't have to make all the changes at once. For the best outcomes, pick just one thing. Otherwise, if there are too many changes made at once, you can become confused. It conflicts with the desire to develop into a more self-controlled person.

Improve your self-control. Self-discipline is a learned talent; we do not naturally possess it. To learn it, you must train daily, just like you would with any other skill.

It takes a lot of effort to develop self-discipline and dedication, just like going to the gym. The effort and concentration required for self-discipline can be draining.

It will get harder and harder to control your willpower as time goes on. It may be more challenging to complete some jobs that also need self-control the greater the incentive or choice. Work diligently and continuously to hone your self-discipline.

Determine what you want to change. Even so, do you enjoy kale smoothies? Desire to be? Even if drinking one might seem like a good, healthy thing to do, it won't make you a better person. But if you just do it for the wrong reasons, it can turn you into an unbearable jerk. When focusing on fitness, pick a doable activity that will significantly improve your life, and, ideally, that you enjoy. Going to the gym, using the stairs rather than the elevator, or limiting your ice cream consumption are a few examples.

Keep things straightforward to develop new habits.
Learning self-discipline and trying to establish a new habit can first seem daunting, especially if you focus on the entire work at hand. Just keep things straightforward to prevent feeling threatened. Divide your goal into manageable, quick steps. Focus on consistently doing one thing and exercise self-discipline with that goal in mind rather than trying to change everything at once. Start by working out for 10 to 15 minutes each day if you want to get in shape. Start each night by retiring 15 minutes earlier if you want to develop better sleep habits. Continue eating your lunch the night before you take it with you in the morning if you want to eat healthily. Get moving for the boy.

Finally, when you are able, you can include new objectives on your list. It's true that feeling angry—the dissatisfied, dejected, and irritated feelings you experience when you're hungry—can have a big impact on your ability to resist temptation. Low blood sugar levels have been demonstrated to undermine a person's resolve and make them irritable and pessimistic.

When you're hungry, your ability to concentrate decreases, and your brain doesn't function as well. There is no doubt that you have less self-control in all areas, including eating, exercising, working, and interacting with others. To maintain control, you fill up with wholesome snacks and frequent meals.

Modify how you think about willpower. According to a Stanford University investigation, a person's beliefs impact how much willpower they have. When you are aware of your limited willpower, you are less likely to go above those limits. You're less likely to kill yourself until you accomplish your goals if you don't place a cap on your self-control. In other words, our internal beliefs about our capacity for self-control and willpower determine how much we have of both.

Make a List Part of self-discipline. Self-discipline is realizing what you need to do, and then doing it. If you can overcome these latent barriers and truly believe you can, then you will be giving yourself an extra boost in inspiration to make your ambitions a reality. When you're not used to acting in a disciplined manner, it can be difficult to think of your next duty. Make a list of the tasks you need to complete before you start the day.

You should schedule personal activities or include work-related duties in your daily agenda. The agenda can include everything, including emails, laundry, and grocery store trips. Building self-discipline will help you cross items off the list.

Make decisions beforehand. Leave your phone at your workplace if your goal is to maintain patience during sessions. Also, don't put it in your pocket. It cannot be played with if it is not present. Ask the server to wrap half of your lunch in front of you if you want to develop better self-control around food, or limit your consumption to half of the sandwich at all times. Decide how many emails you will be listening to before doing anything else if you want to stay on top of your inbox, whether it's five, ten, or all. Deciding in advance can make it much simpler for you to resist temptation when it arrives.

Use Technology. Because people can always search on Facebook, Twitter, or Snapchat in addition to playing games and finding partners, technology makes consumers transient. Technical tools, however, can also aid in the development of the discipline.

Additionally, you can set timers to limit how much time you spend online or on your time-sucking website. They can utilize one that tracks your time and gives you a sense of how you are using it, and then they can use that information to figure out how to cut down on the amount of time you waste.

Establish a backup strategy. To increase motivation, psychologists employ a strategy called "implementation goals." At that point, you present yourself with a strategy to handle a potentially difficult circumstance that you are likely to encounter. Consider the scenario where you want to eat healthily but are en route to a gathering where food will be served.

Before you go, focus on mixing and tell yourself that you will be sipping water rather than devouring a plate of cheese and crackers. Having a plan can help you approach the circumstance with the right attitude and level of restraint. Additionally, you'll save time by avoiding an impulsive emotional choices.

Praise yourself. When you create a reward for reaching your goals, give yourself something to be excited about. Getting something to look forward to offers you the motivation to be productive, just as when you were a young boy.

Expectations are high. This provides you with something to think about and focus on, helping you to stop worrying about the things you're attempting to alter. When you accomplish that objective, you will discover a new target and a fresh motivation to keep going.

Forgive yourself, then proceed. Despite our greatest efforts and well-laid strategies, we still fall short. It does occur. There will be highs and lows, notable victories, and heartbreaking losses. The secret is to keep running. If you find yourself faltering, consider what set it off and continue. Remorse, hatred, or disappointment should not consume you since they will only make you feel worse and prevent you from moving forward. Forgive others and learn from your mistakes. Then return to the game and concentrate on your objectives.

Keep in mind that failure is a necessary component of success. The majority of people desire to develop self-control, but after making a mistake on day two, they give up on their intended timetable. You won't achieve perfect organization right away, and you'll allow some relapses to occur. Nevertheless, if you prepare for it and understand that you will occasionally fail, one setback won't ruin your entire strategy for success. At the same time, you must celebrate your victories. All five of the objectives you set for yourself this week have been met. Repay the debt and celebrate in a way that won't degrade your achievement. Let's say that your company's objective is to attract new clients. A poor reward would be to take three days off from prospecting. A satisfying reward can be lunch with a friend at a posh eatery. The improvement of your self-discipline will affect all areas of your life. Pick one field to begin with if you're ready to go.

Remain Conscious of Your Feelings at All Times
You have begun to build your emotional awareness when you routinely take the time to acknowledge how you feel. People often neglect their thoughts and feelings due to the stress of the day, which causes a variety of unfavorable emotions to flourish in their hearts and minds and generate elevated levels of tension and anxiety.

When someone comes home from a very stressful day at work, even the smallest trigger can send them over the edge. How frequently have you let your anxiety and rage affect how you interact with others? Some people experience this issue repeatedly because they lack emotional awareness and are extremely weak.

You are better able to manage your social interactions when you are emotionally aware. Asking a random question about your feelings is the first step. Most of the time, you'll be able to answer right away; it might be worry, exhaustion, or even happiness and relaxation.

Whatever the emotion, it's critical to be cognizant of it. You pause to consider the best way to handle these emotions after determining your emotional condition. Pause if you need to calm down or if you are anxious or irritated. You can lower the tension you are currently experiencing by going for a walk, listening to music, or talking to a loved one. Regularly doing this helps you manage your emotions and prevents tension and rage.

Between the Lines Reading

Other indicators of how someone else may be feeling exist. These are the bodily arousal indicators that you are aware of in yourself. People may be experiencing practically any powerful emotion when they begin to breathe more quickly without any apparent cause. They could feel scared if they start to sweat all of a sudden. They may feel embarrassed, furious, ashamed, or guilty when their face gets crimson. They may be scared or angry if their face turns white.

The way someone speaks can also say a lot about them. People frequently begin speaking louder and more quickly when they are angry, scared, or thrilled. The tone of their voice may also rise in times of rage or terror. Conversely, people who are depressed or bored could speak more slowly and softly. Their voice pitch may also be dropped when they are unhappy. There is also body language. People that are confident and driven convey these qualities by standing up straight and tall. When people bend in your direction while you're speaking, they're expressing interest. They are demonstrating the contrary when they fidget and tap their fingers. And if they give you a direct look, they're probably being truthful.

Try this experiment to see how much you can infer from body language and facial emotions alone: Put the sound on mute and spend a few minutes watching a drama or comedy on TV. Try to infer from people's looks and gestures which emotions they are trying to convey. Once the sound is playing, check to see how correct your predictions were. You will likely be able to infer certain emotions from others without hearing a single word that they say.

People might be able to learn to mimic some of these signals. Of course, it would be exceedingly challenging to pull off all of them at once. Let's say that despite not wearing it recently, you discover a new stain on your beloved T-shirt. You assume that your sister unintentionally ruined the shirt by wearing it while you weren't looking. She looks you in the eye when you inquire about it, and she immediately denies it. Her face however gets red at the same time. You conclude that she might be remorseful.

That could be the case. On the other hand, your sister might be upset that you don't trust her and be blushing as a result. It's not as simple as reading this book to learn how to read people's emotions. It's more akin to deciphering a difficult mystery. Typically, no one piece of information can give the entire story. Instead, it's a matter of assembling all the information and seeking out the best plausible explanation.

Implementing an Individual's Emotions

Once you have mastered the art of reading people's emotions, you are in a prime position to change how they feel. To persuade someone to buy an idea, product, plan, or concept, you might need to play on their emotions. Sometimes manipulating someone's emotions might help them become a better person.

An angry or unhappy individual may need to be made joyful to be more productive. It's critical to develop your ability to read other people's emotions so that you can comprehend them more fully. For instance, you can decide if someone needs to be left alone or needs someone to talk to by understanding the type of terrible mood they are in.

To better influence the person you are seeking to understand, you must establish an alliance with them. If both of you are headed in the same direction, it will be simpler to go there together; however, if you do anything to make someone feel awful, they are less likely to listen to you. Although social competence is a vast topic, it is properly employed in emotional intelligence. In the context of emotional intelligence, social skills are the capacity to manage and shape other people's emotions successfully. Understanding your emotions and controlling them wisely will help you achieve your goals. Once you have mastered your own emotions, you can easily control those of others. The following actions can help you develop your social skills and raise your emotional intelligence:

Communication skills
Emotional intelligence includes a critical component called communication skills. People with strong emotional intelligence are better at listening to others and expressing their feelings in appropriate ways. A competent communicator pays close attention to what others are saying and comprehends the message being delivered. This provides kids

the freedom to interpret and respond to emotional cues to behave appropriately.

Develop your conflict resolution abilities

Disagreements and conflicts are a natural element of human existence. Emotional intelligence is crucial for success in both your personal and professional life. One significant part of emotional intelligence is the capacity to resolve arguments in challenging situations. You can manage conflict successfully after you understand the value of diplomacy and tact.

Boost your leadership abilities

Emotional intelligence and leadership go hand in hand. If you want to influence a leader, you must be able to control your emotions. One of the qualities of a strong leader is their capacity for visual communication as well as their capacity to hold others accountable while offering support and advice.

Learn how to influence and persuade

Motivating others and persuading them to do your bidding are key components of persuasion. You may convince folks to enroll in your course with ease if you have good emotional intelligence. They can gauge the emotional climate at any given moment and modify their reaction to suit all audiences.

Work on forming strong relationships

Establishing and maintaining healthy relationships is a crucial component of gaining emotional intelligence. Your connections will improve and your motivation to move forward in life will increase if you have this skill. People who are emotionally sophisticated not only form relationships but also work to keep the ones they already have.

Stop Overthinking

Change begins with awareness. You must be aware of it every time you are conscious of it before you can begin to confront or cope with your tendency of overthinking. When things are tough or you're feeling apprehensive or stressed out, take a step back and evaluate what happened and how you responded. In that instant of awareness lies the seed of the change you wish to see.

Consider what could go right rather than what could go wrong. Panic is the one emotion that frequently causes overthinking. When you focus on all the worst scenarios that could occur, it's simple to become stuck. The next time you sense yourself heading in that direction, halt. Consider all the positive possibilities, and keep those emotions present and in the present.

Divert your attention to make you happy. It can be helpful at times to find enjoyable, upbeat, healthful alternatives to pass the time. Meditation, music, exercise, playing an instrument, knitting, writing, and painting are some activities that can stop you from over-analyzing your difficulties.

Adjust your perspective. It is always quick to make things bigger and more negative than they need to be. The next time you see yourself constructing a mountain out of a molehill, stop and consider how important it will be in five years. For that matter, simply next month. By altering the timetable, just asking this straightforward question can stop overthinking.

Give up expecting perfection. Simply put, all of us who are currently anticipating greatness may stop waiting. Being positive is great, but striving for perfection is unachievable, unattainable, and crippling. You need to understand that waiting for the best is never as intellectually stimulating as moving forward the instant you start thinking, "This must be wonderful."

Modify how you perceive fear. Remember that just because something didn't work out in the past doesn't indicate that it has to happen every time. This is true whether you're afraid of attempting because you've failed in the past, or you're afraid of failing because you're overgeneralizing some other loss. Remember that every opportunity is a new beginning and a chance to start over.

Start the timer. Set boundaries for yourself. Set a five-minute timer and give yourself the space to reflect, mull, and assess. With a pen and paper, take ten minutes after the timer goes off to list all the things that worry you, bother you, or are causing you anxiety. Let loose. Throw the paper aside after the ten minutes are up and move on to something enjoyable, preferably.

Accept that you cannot foretell the future. Nobody can foretell the future; we only have the present. You are currently depriving yourself of your time if you are thinking about the future in the present. Simply put, investing in the future is unsuccessful. Spend that time on activities that will make you happy instead. Accepting your best, the dread of overanalyzing causes is frequently centered on the idea that you're not strong enough—not smart enough, not hard-working enough, not devoted enough. When you've given it your all, recognize it for what it is and recognize that even though the outcome may depend in part on factors outside your control, you've done everything you could.

Show gratitude. Why not make the most of the time by doing something constructive instead of thinking about regrets and being happy at the same time? Make a list of your blessings every morning and every night. To have a monument to the good things around you, make a friend with thanks and exchange lists. Overthinking is one thing that can happen to everybody. However, if you have a good system in place, you can at least ward off some of the gloomy, anxious, and overpowering ideas and channel them into something effective, efficient, and positive.

Visualizing Your Goals: A Guide

Success in life and work begins with a goal. It can be losing weight, looking for a job, giving up smoking, or launching your own business. Objectives, no matter how great or small, provide us with direction and give our lives meaning. Of all, it takes a lot of effort and perseverance to get where you're going.

Aristotle outlined the steps in his writings more than 2,000 years ago. He said, "First, have a real, simple, realistic ideal; an aim, a target; second, have the means necessary to achieve your ends: knowledge, resources, tools, and procedures. Third, adjust all of your means to do it. Sadly, a lot of us are still unable to move past the goal.

We have good intentions at first and sometimes even a plan, but eventually, it seems impossible to make things happen. Career, impatience, worry, and unfavorable social variables are only a few of the regular offenders. How do we respond to these difficulties and move closer to our objective?

Knowing by doing

Before we can believe in a mission, we must first grasp what it feels like. We have to see it before we believe, to paraphrase an old proverb. This is where simulation, which is essentially a method for visualizing a possible event, starts. As we visualize our ideal outcome, we begin to "read" the likelihood of reaching it. According to one study, we may envision our "ideal future" by using our imagination. When this occurs, we are motivated and equipped to accomplish our objectives.

Visualization is not the same as the advice to "say it and be it," which is promoted by well-known self-help gurus. It is not a ruse, nor is it a wish for a better tomorrow. Instead, visualization is a well-established performance improvement technique supported by reliable scientific data and utilized by successful people in a range of fields.

Let's start with the athletes. According to research, using one's imagination increases motivation, cohesiveness, and focus during athletic competition. Additionally, it promotes calmness, which lessens fear and anxiety. According to one researcher, "the athlete only does it and does it with faith, composure, and precision" when they see something. Jerry West, a legendary NBA star, is a fantastic illustration of how this occurs. He earned the moniker "Mr. Clutch" due to his propensity for making jumpers at the buzzer.

West explained that he had practiced making those identical shots countless times in his head before being asked what made up for his ability to make the big shots. Numerous athletes, like Tiger Woods, Larry Bird, Michael Jordan, and pitcher Roy Halladay, used simulation to enhance their performance and achieve their personal best.

Why Visualization Is Effective

According to research employing brain imaging, visualization is effective because neurons in our brains—those electrically excitable cells that transmit information—perceive it as being equivalent to a real-life action. When we visualize performing an activity, the brain sends an impulse that causes our neurons to "perform" the action.

This establishes a new neural route, which in turn primes our body to behave in a way consistent with our expectations. Neural pathways are cell clusters in our brains that collaborate to construct memories or acquired patterns. All of this happens without actually engaging in physical exercise, but the result is the same.

How Does It Function?

Visualization is only the act of creating an image in your head of a future situation. As the adage goes, we must see it for it to be done. It's a tried-and-true method of achieving our goals. Visualization awakens the creative subconscious, which contributes to the development of fresh approaches to greater goals. This activates the law of attraction, which states that success requires the appropriate circumstances, goods, and people.

Additionally, imagination encourages us to take the actions required to accomplish goals by facilitating internal drive. In reality, research done by Russia has demonstrated that simulation is more than just a hoax and that it can assist Olympic athletes to compete. The study examined four different Olympian classes that each spent a specific amount of time working on their physical and mental health.

Groups one through four all engage in 100% physical training, 75% physical training and 25% mental training, 50% physical training and 50% mental training, and 25% physical training and 75% mental training, respectively.
Surprisingly, researchers discovered that the fourth group fared best during the Olympic Games. While doing the physical action, participants were found to be using the same brain regions that are engaged by fantasy. The brain is better able to work toward reaching goals thanks to this straightforward yet effective strategy.

How to picture
Simply defined, imagination begins by establishing a goal, then deeply considering achieving that objective, and finally meditating on it over an extended period. Anyone can employ one or more of the several strategies for the imagination to better reach their objectives. Sitting with your eyes closed and viewing oneself in as much detail as you can in one vision is a basic method. As you do this, try to picture yourself having achieved the goal. You should allot a brief time every day or many days a week to fit this workout into your routine.

Message boards

Many people also adhere to this technique of animation, in which a person collects images from newspapers and publications that represent their goals before assembling them into a collage.

Affirmations

Affirmations assist establish goals and boost confidence regularly. Use uplifting affirmations to motivate you and break down any barriers keeping you from living the life you want. For instance, a person who feels undeserving of love should tell themselves aloud each morning, "I love myself. My friends and family are great to me. I merit your love.

Goals list

By putting our expectations in writing, we can focus on what we want and take steps to achieve it. You should either focus on a small number of significant objectives or compile a lengthy list of at least 25 wants on a weekly or monthly basis. Should you restrict your life's options? Imagine an ideal life and achieve what seems unattainable, no matter how impossible it may seem.

Bringing Everything Together

Don't forget that you don't have to be an outstanding athlete to gain from the simulation. Visualization will keep you focused on your goal and improve your chances of achieving it, whether you're a student, investor, parent, or spouse. Everyone has the capacity for imagination.

There are two types of visualization, each serving a different purpose, but for the best results, they should be combined. The first strategy involves simulating the outcome and visualizing oneself achieving the objective. Use all of your senses to build a complete mental picture of the desired outcome as you accomplish this. If your goal is to complete your first marathon, for instance, picture yourself at the finish line. As long as you can, hold the image in your head.

What does it feel like to cross the finish line while looking at your phone and feeling the chilly breeze on your sweaty body? When you're finished, who will greet you? Your family? Friends? Other athletes? Imagine the thrill, joy, and rush you'll experience as you finally emerge from the lactic acid and pass out in their arms. Many people find it helpful to write down their goal in as much detail as they can, then translate it into a graphic depiction. It could be a flowchart, an image, or a hand-drawn drawing. Public opinion is irrelevant as long as it aids in your ability to develop a distinct mental identity and maintain inspiration.

The simulation of systems is the second sort of visualization. It involves picturing every action necessary to get the desired goal. Instead of thinking about the objective itself, consider every action you need to take to achieve it.

Consider the marathon again: Before the race, picture yourself running with your arms relaxed, your breathing steady, and your legs pumping like pistons. Imagine how each segment of the route should proceed, breaking it down into manageable portions while considering your speed, gait, and split time. When you reach "the wall," the part of the journey where your body wants to give up, picture how it will seem and, more importantly, consider what you must do to push through.

You are not capable of competing in a marathon. However, the same principles can be applied to achieve any goal: create a clear mental vision of your success, plan out each stage of the process, and employ motivational imagery, such as an athlete racing through "the stone," to keep focused and motivated as you encounter obstacles or failures. Success is not always visualized. It doesn't take the place of discipline and hard effort. However, when combined with focused effort (and, in my opinion, a solid support system), it is a powerful strategy for bringing about positive behavioral change and creating the life you want.

Surround Yourself with Positive People to Help You Recognize Negative Influences and Habits. Both the individuals we choose to spend time with and the people we are compelled to see can have a profound effect on us. When you begin to believe the awful things that other people say, you will begin to internalize their comments.

Maybe you can name at least one person in your life who makes you regret ever knowing them. Keep them off your thoughts; it's sometimes the greatest thing you can do. However, you may not always be able to accomplish that. At work or home, there will inevitably be a lot of people. Therefore, in addition to ending toxic relationships, you should learn how to manage them and find new, more fulfilling connections to take their place.

As soon as you decide that being alone is preferable for you, make sure you're sure that's the proper course to take. It's challenging to recover from that severe action, and there's a chance that your friendship won't be mended. If someone is a friend, severing ties with them is simpler. You don't need to associate with people who know them or dress in the same way as your peers or peers of theirs. It is your choice whether or not to maintain a partner close by. You can choose, for instance, the family member you want in your life. Just be sure you take the proper action and oust anyone who is callous, inconsiderate, or disrespectful.

There will probably be some unfavorable folks. You might have difficult coworkers, your best friend's obnoxious wife, or a significant relative you must see over the holidays. If you can't or don't want to eliminate someone from your life, you will learn how to deal with them more skillfully. If you don't, you can find that their opinions have an impact on your life.

You can cope with the kind of individual who seems to only have negative things to say in a variety of ways. Despite what they are telling you, one is to simply smile and leave. However, in other circumstances, such as at work, you cannot use that form. When you need to stay involved, try to encourage them by using encouraging words.

Keep in mind to concentrate on your resources and that their issue is their unfavorable attitude. Make sure to counterbalance any negative influences in your life with more uplifting ones when you are under pressure to surrounding yourself with them. Choose to be with positive people, and use your positivity to counteract others' negativity.

Modifying Your Way of Life. They are not the only item that has the potential to significantly affect your life.

It is quite simple to develop undesirable habits that let the rulers influence you. If you take a close look at your lifestyle, you can discover that you are depending on something that has begun to dictate how you live. If you acknowledge and make an effort to control such addictions, you can become a healthier and more self-assured individual. It makes no difference if you need to start a detox program, improve your eating habits, or seek help for alcohol addiction.

Nothing should control your life such that you feel compelled to do anything, even if it makes you unhappy. Change some bad behaviors to positive ones, such as your food, social life, and a wide range of interests.

You need to make other lifestyle changes if you want to start thinking more positively. If your thoughts are bad as a result of the situation, changing the situation may be far easier than altering your thoughts. Start looking for a new job if your current one causes you stress and you keep making mistakes because of it. Deal with the issues that are dictating your life, then start planning how you will change things going forward.

Fighting against negative thinking. Only if you adopt a more positive mindset and learn how to deal with unfavorable thoughts can you alter your way of life. Positive people can be stopped, but you also need to take a closer look at yourself. One of the best things you can do to better your life is to set goals and objectives so that you have something to work for. But you need to examine your thought processes if you want to stay on course. To help you identify the source of the issue, you can look at where your ideas and emotions originate when you think negatively. Thoughts or experiences that are unfavorable cannot entirely be eliminated, you can decide to concentrate on the positive.

Whatever happens to you, no matter how insignificant it may be, you should learn from it. Even though you may have had a horrible day, someone was considerate enough to hold a door open for you when you arrived at work. You haven't been able to drop much weight for a long, but you have stuck to your diet plan and avoided the forbidden foods. Celebrate the good and battle the bad by not letting them control your life, according to the philosophy of positive thinking.

Management of Anxiety
Reduce Your Coffee Consumption

In beverages produced with coffee, tea, chocolate, and energy, caffeine is a stimulant. Anxiety will be heightened with high doses. The amount of caffeine that each person can tolerate varies. Consider reducing your caffeine intake if you find it makes you jittery or anxious. Although numerous studies have shown that coffee can be fairly decent, not everyone like it. Most people regard five cups or fewer per day to be a moderate amount. Pencil it down

Writing down ideas is one method of releasing tension.

One approach is to write down your worries, while another is to make a list of your blessings. By keeping your mind on the positive aspects of your life, gratitude can assist to reduce stress and worry. Consider chewing a stick of gum as an incredibly simple and fast stress reliever.

According to one study, those who chew gum feel healthier and have less discomfort.

One possibility is that chewing gum causes brain waves that are comparable to those of relaxed persons. Gum that promotes blood flow to the brain is another option. Additionally, a recent study discovered that persons who chewed more ferociously experienced the most stress reduction.

Spend time with family and friends. You'll need social support from friends and family to get through these trying times. Having a network of friends provides you with a sense of identity and worth that can help you through trying times. Spending time with friends and children, particularly for women, helps release oxytocin, a natural stress reliever, according to one study.

The opposite of the fight-or-flight response is the "tend and mate" effect. Remember that friendship has advantages for both men and women. According to the study, those with the fewest social connections—both men and women—were more likely to experience melancholy and anxiety.

Laugh

It's difficult to be anxious while you're grinning. It is beneficial to your health and can reduce stress in a few different ways. Reducing the way you react to stress. Relaxing the muscles to release stress. Long-term humor can strengthen the mood and immune system. In a study of cancer patients, participants who received a laughter intervention reported less stress than those who were only distracted. Try to find a humorous television program to watch, or spend time with people who make you laugh.

Practice saying no

Some stressors are under your control, but not all of them are. Become in charge of the aspects of your life that need to change and are stressful. Saying "no" more frequently might be one approach to do it. This is particularly true if you discover that you are taking on more than you can manage because juggling will leave you feeling overburdened by numerous duties.

Stress levels can be decreased by being picky about what you take on and declining offers that will simply increase your workload.

Recognize and combat procrastination

Maintaining focus on your priorities and quitting procrastination are additional ways to control your emotions. You may have to work hard to catch up if you procrastinate since reactive action may result. This may lead to stress, which harms your health and sleep. Establish the practice of creating prioritized to-do lists. Set realistic deadlines for yourself as you move down the list.

Give yourself uninterrupted time and concentrate on the tasks you must complete right away because switching between tasks or multitasking itself might be challenging.

Attend a yoga lesson

Yoga has become a popular form of exercise and stress treatment for people of all ages. Although there are many different styles of yoga, they all aim to help you reconnect with your body and mind. Yoga accomplishes this mostly by raising body and breath awareness. Numerous studies have examined yoga's effects on mental health. Overall, studies have shown that yoga can elevate mood and may even be just as successful in treating anxiety and depression as antidepressant drugs. However, many of these data are inconclusive, and it is still unclear how yoga helps people reduce stress.

Yoga's benefit for reducing stress and anxiety appears to often be related to how it affects your neurological system and how you respond to stress. Gamma-aminobutyric acid (GABA), a neurotransmitter that is decreased in mood disorders, may be increased, and it may also help lower cortisol levels, blood pressure, and heart rate.

Develop mindfulness

Mindfulness is a set of techniques that keeps you focused on the present. It may assist to counteract the anxiety-inducing consequences of gloomy thinking. From attention-based stress reduction, yoga, and meditation to mindfulness-based cognitive treatment, there are many techniques to raise consciousness. According to a recent study conducted on college students, being careful may boost one's self-esteem, which in turn lessens the symptoms of worry and melancholy.

Cuddle up

Tension can be reduced by hugging, kissing, massaging, and sexual activity. Positive physical touch can help with the release of oxytocin and reduce the release of cortisol. This can aid in reducing heart rate and blood pressure, both of which are signs of physical stress. Ironically, animals aren't the only ones who cuddle up to relax after a stressful day. Chimpanzees also comfort distressed pals by cuddling.

Play Relaxing Music

The body can be greatly calmed by listening to music. Instrumental music that is played slowly can induce relaxation by reducing stress hormones, blood pressure, and heart rate. While it can be very relaxing to listen to some types of classical, Celtic, Native American, and Indian music, it can also be very effective to just play the music you enjoy. Natural noises can also be incredibly calming.

Breathing deeply

The sympathetic nervous system is activated by mental stress, indicating that your body is entering the "fight or flight" response. During this response, stress hormones are released, and you experience bodily symptoms like a faster heartbeat, faster breathing and closed blood vessels.

Deep breathing exercises can help your parasympathetic nervous system, which regulates the body's response to relaxation, come into action.

There are many different deep breathing methods, such as synchronized breathing, diaphragmatic breathing, abdominal breathing, and belly breathing. Deep breathing aims to focus your attention on your breathing, making it faster and deeper. Your lungs fully expand and your abdomen expands as you inhale deeply via your nose. Your heart rate will slow down, as a result, making you feel more at ease.

Time Spent With Your Pet

Having a pet can help you feel happier and less stressed. Interacting with animals can aid in the release of oxytocin, a brain hormone that promotes a happy mood. By giving you purpose, keeping you active, and providing companionship—all of which lessen anxiety—having a pet can also help alleviate depression.

DECIPHERING THOUGHTS

Maybe you've previously been mesmerized by a mind reading on television or in person. We frequently ponder how such a "wonderful man" can know things that are impossible for him to know. Does he possess psychic powers, or is this all simply a clever ruse to con us? What's the key to it? I can guarantee you in advance one thing: These demonstrations have nothing to do with any extraterrestrial abilities.

However, the mind reader creates the appearance that he can read the minds of other people. And he makes an impression on us. What is the cause of the alleged miracles? Simple: although we are unknown to them, several communication methods give the appearance that you know everything about a person. It involves rigorous observation on the one hand, as well as understanding human nature and intuition, on the other. So let's look at the mentalists' backstage areas.

Signals made by the body

Many people think that body language analysis and interpretation are the only methods used in mind reading. Therefore, to eventually deduce the thoughts of one's counterpart, one would need to constantly monitor his body language and evaluate all conceivable readings against one another.

In reality, this is not always attainable because different arm and hand gestures might convey diverse messages, making it impossible to generalize how body language should be perceived. It takes time to examine and comprehend body language. If you go through it too carefully, you run the risk of losing focus on the real dialogue and possibly even becoming lost in your thoughts. There is no doubt that business negotiations would not benefit from this.

However, if you know how to monitor human behavior, body language can offer important cues that are simple to find. The following signals frequently show up in meetings and conversations and indicate particular ideas, so it is helpful to be aware of them.

Gnaw on your lips

Biting one's lips is a sign that one is trying to delay saying something they don't want to say. a symptom of either low confidence or humiliation. You may now infer what the other person is feeling and thinking based on the circumstance. Biting his lips indicates that he is searching for the right words to say what he is feeling, such as if he was caught doing something embarrassing. Giving him something he can affirm will make it simpler for him to communicate his genuine thoughts. So, one response may be, "I can understand that this is uncomfortable for you and you are unsure how to communicate it." If it appears more useful to avoid the issue, you can also shift the subject.

Inhale

Swallowing is another sign that pressure is building up inside of you because you feel trapped or see-through. You simply want to make what happened disappear, so you swallow it. An instinctive effort to get out of unfavorable circumstances there are several options for handling this scenario as well.

Tightened lips

Lips are locked together in a lock. The opposing party is unwilling to receive any facts since it might stick with its position and avoid trying something new. You can communicate the other person's viewpoint if you detect this reaction, for instance during a sales call, by expressing "I suspect you do not agree with me" or "You probably see it differently."

Hand on cheek

A person is attentively assessing what is happening or what has been heard if they place their hand on their cheek. He is therefore concerned about the current circumstance. I can see that you need to think about it first, and he'll probably agree with that.

Sweep your chin.

This response conveys a similar message. The distinction is that a decision-making process is currently underway. Both movements frequently overlap. The chin is reached after the hand has first been put on the cheek. Sometimes the motion is accompanied by a brief sniff or a "Hmm..." In this instance, it is true that "It is important to you to take into account all factors before you make a decision."

Hands-on hips

When the hands are supported on the hips, it frequently indicates aggression. Typically, the hip is pushed forward while the head is pulled back. Due to the extended elbows, this posture stabilizes you and gives you a wider appearance. In a metaphorical sense, this indicates that you are now ready and willing to battle. Someone who has their hands on their hips can confront another person, but they may also be anticipating a verbal attack, and their stance suggests that they won't give an inch.

In this situation, it's crucial to pay closer attention. If the former is true, it is up to each individual to decide how much they want to participate in this circumstance. In the second situation, which can happen, for instance, when you face someone with a change and they respond by placing their hands on their hips, you can tell that they will find it challenging to shift their point of view. It makes sense to respond to him and demonstrate understanding, for instance by saying: "I would probably react precisely like you," to lessen the tension.

Holding hands

The interlocutor is showing signs of fear if he grips the chair armrest, the edge of the table, or any of the things on the table. He reaches for anything to grasp, reduce doubt, and find support. There are various reasons for fear. You should exude confidence and composure as long as you are unsure of its source before advancing cautiously toward the background.

Clapping hands

Someone is impatient when they beat their fingers against the table. He simply moves too slowly, and he wants to quicken the process. Feet can be seesawed or the chair can be moved back and forth to add to this motion. The causes change based on the circumstances. He can B. ask you to finish your speech sooner. I think that's moving too slowly for you, you said. Then hits the mark. Let's get right to the point.

Input nose

Lying is indicated by touching or scratching your nose. Blood pressure rises and the body releases chemical messages while one is lying down. The result is swelling of the nasal mucous membranes, which irritates. Nose-scratching is not usually a sign of deception. Anybody who has a cold would have to be suspected otherwise. The itching typically occurs more frequently when a lie is told. When you see this movement, you should pay attention. It is frequently incidental and barely identifiable. It's time to ask more specific and apply a little more pressure. You will then be able to detect if the other person is lying to you or telling the truth based on the circumstances.

Eyes should be rubbed.

When they don't want to see something, children automatically cover their eyes with their hands. Adults can also be seen engaging in this practice. It is not as obvious here, though. One only lightly touches the palm in the eye, not covering the eyes. It demonstrates that the speaker is uncertain. "You are highly critical and cannot fully believe what I am saying," might be a suitable response.

Grab your nose

When lying down, touching the nose is different from this gesture. The fingers are pressing against the nose bridge while the head is slightly dropped. The eyes are frequently shut. This response, which might be brief, expresses the interlocutor's negative assessment of what has just occurred or been discussed. The other person is more focused on their internal view, as evidenced by closed eyes. You can directly address the issue by saying, "I assume you are unsatisfied," to get a sense of what the other person is thinking.

Jerk the ear

Pulling on your ear can be a sign of uncertainty. Typically, the head is lowered slightly. If you allow your rival z. The discussion partner is highly likely to be confused if, for instance, you select one of the numerous possibilities and the other person then realizes that your ear is pulling. You feel conflicted and are unsure of what to do, which is likely a good description of the other person's thoughts. However, if you tell someone anything and they pull your ear, it usually signifies that they've had enough and want to add something.

Observe the earth

A person's hostility toward the views put forward is evident if they avoid eye contact and instead maintain their gaze on the floor during a discourse. Fear often exhibits physical symptoms. If the person you are speaking with exhibits this response after you have offered a recommendation, it can be helpful to respond with, "I can see that sometimes it is not easy to get involved with something new.

One method to understand the thinking of the other person is to watch for these body language cues. As a result, instead of searching for them, you should react to them as soon as you see them. In the absence of this, you run the danger of overlooking other significant hints or even getting lost in a "body language study."

Fishing

Inquiring about details is a useful and successful strategy for understanding what your opponent is thinking. The individual you are speaking to usually starts to tell you more about themselves, especially if you two have developed a solid rapport. This method resembles a questionnaire in many ways. However, the "respondent" does not feel as though he is responding to inquiries; rather, he feels as though he is being understood. You can get him to open up by fishing for more information.

Fishing is a really easy activity. Instead of posing a question to the interviewee, you express it as a statement, make it public, and then watch for his response. This demonstrates whether the claim was accurate and how to move forward. If you do this effectively, the other person will naturally link and consider how the comment might be interpreted. He won't overlook it or lose track of who provided the information.

By "continuing to fish" at this point, the feedback is used to rectify any inaccurate statements or to affirm and reinforce correct statements. This creates the idea that you are prepared and that you are aware of everything about the person you are speaking to.

Provide criticism

Creating a question that is also a statement is the first step in fishing. Be careful not to commit yourself too quickly. It is comparable to cooking seasoning. Sprinkle pepper, salt, and other spices sparingly, then taste and adjust the seasoning to your liking. If you season the cuisine excessively from the beginning, you cannot reduce the salt content. The same holds for remarks made while fishing. Until you have the chance of a guaranteed hit, you should word it so that you are still keeping another path open.

Then and only then do you spice things up or add more. In this manner, you drop hints while gradually getting closer to the essence. You have very little chance of failing if you start building things too soon. You can respond,

"I have the sensation that you are not truly pleased yet," if you notice, for instance, that the other person is tentative and restrained as you are presenting something to him.

I haven't given a justification or stated a definitive fact like "you're not satisfied." You can omit a specific date in favor of phrases like "recent" or "shortly" to avoid committing yourself to a specific moment.

Even though "recent" might refer to anything that happened only recently, it can also refer to something that happened months or even years ago. Our counterpart lengthens it like a rubber band by pulling it to the proper length. The same holds for "shortly after." However, only in a week, a month, or a year might that imply tomorrow. "Soon," "in the past," "recently," "in the future," and "for a time" are more examples of "rubber band" words.

Avoiding gender-specific terms is beneficial in addition to timing issues. The more impartial you are at the outset, the more equipped you will be to respond to your conversation partner as the talk progresses.

You can use the subjunctive to vague phrasing to soften your claims. Using phrases like "maybe" or "maybe" does not commit you to anything, and you can always back down later if you are mistaken. Other suitable openings include "I get the impression that..." "I feel ..." "My impression is that..." "I get the feeling that..." It's similar to...

There are times when speculating is advantageous. Simply said, you shouldn't be afraid to be incorrect. You can achieve excellent results by carefully considering what is most likely to fit and hazarding a guess. Naturally, you should consider your hypotheses and ultimately only declare those that have the best chance of being accurate.

In the best-case scenario, having a presupposition based on facts is a great approach to starting a dialogue, explaining them, and relying on luck. Since the next statements will be accepted considerably sooner if this one is true, you will immediately receive a hit that fits exactly. Further inferences can be made from the counterpart's answers, which will likewise be more transparent and comprehensible. There are ways to make the claim a hit even if you are incorrect and carry on fishing. It's crucial to pause after commenting and refrain from saying or doing anything else. This puts a little pressure on your opponent. The pressure on your discussion partner is released if you talk more or move around restlessly. Therefore, in this circumstance, it is advisable to momentarily "freeze." The other person will yield to pressure and respond to you to receive feedback. After that, you proceed.

Receive criticism

Feedback usually comes after you have made the statement and taken a moment to reflect. There are essentially three possibilities. The assertion is true in the ideal and initial scenario. If you are slightly off in the second scenario, the assertion is only partially true. The third possibility is that the statement is a complete failure due to your error.

Now, the speaker has several options for expressing his acceptance or disapproval. When speaking in ordinary communication, this happens frequently. This implies that a hit frequently returns a "yes" response. However, a comparable response is also typical. On the flip side, you get a "No" or a response like, "That's not true." The conversation partner typically pauses as though to remark, "Yes, not quite right," if you are even slightly off. He usually aids in getting the remark correct in casual conversation circumstances.

To infer the other person's genuine ideas, it is important to be aware of the subtle differences between these three distinct groups. For instance, the interlocutor may refute a claim or express skepticism. He can have trouble making up his mind, and he might even disagree with himself. He can also be searching for justifications to avoid owning up to the facts. He may disagree with the statement merely in part. By making observations, you can evaluate where you are.

The Carpenter Effect, also known as the Ideomotor Effect, states that every thought causes a physical response. This depicts the phenomena whereby thinking or imagining a movement causes real, barely noticeable movements. For instance, the concept of a circle causes the pendulum you are holding between your fingers to deflect appropriately.

During my shows, I make use of this occurrence to locate a piece of equipment that the audience has hidden within the crowd. I grab the audience member by the hand and instruct him to focus solely on the direction I should travel. The slightest movements are readily apparent. I know I have to move to the right if I sense a tiny pull to the right. I must go to the left if I detect even a tiny resistance to the right.

However, you may determine if you are correct or incorrect with a statement even without contacting the viewer and solely by observation since when you think "yes," it responds differently from when you think "no." Not only are muscle movements audible, but they are also visual.

You typically nod and move your head reflexively when you, for example, B., agree with someone. On the other hand, a minor head shake can be noticed. Variously, more and less. This occurs entirely unconsciously.

Additionally, the way someone communicates and behaves throughout a conversation is just as crucial as the words they use. How quickly does he communicate? How does he decide what to say and how to react? What pitch does he use when he says it? What stands out about it? Let's say the person you are speaking to response to your comment by saying, "I wouldn't say that this is entirely true."

There are various methods to stress this line, each of which has its meaning and calls attention to a distinct aspect of the text. Depending on whatever word is emphasized, another meaning may be deduced. Often, you can instantly understand what the other person is saying and finish their sentences. I wouldn't say that is entirely accurate. If the word "would not" is highlighted, the other person makes it abundantly obvious that you are utterly mistaken. Here, you need to go around and make the correction.

Later, you'll see exactly how this functions. I wouldn't say that is entirely accurate. If simply "say" is stressed, it's unlikely that the other person will concede that you are correct. It's possible that the assertion was made in a way that makes it truthful, but the interlocutor has trouble verifying it. I wouldn't say that is entirely accurate. The unspoken thinking might have been, "But you're right about the rest." Only "that" was highlighted, therefore it's most likely referring to the previous assertion, which was a miss. The remainder appears to be approved.

There is a good chance that your conversation partner will tell you exactly what was true if you finish your thought and pause. I wouldn't say that is entirely accurate.

The emphasis on "total" has the same meaning as before. The opposing party demonstrates that the majority of the claims presented are true. I wouldn't say that is entirely accurate. If the word "true" is emphasized, you are just off the mark. There is an opportunity for interpretation and speculation in the statements provided. The idea is not at odds with itself. I wouldn't say that is entirely accurate.

The final scenario is that no words are highlighted and the entire speech is monotonously spoken. The speaker might not object to anything individually but might. He acknowledges that there are various viewpoints.

Use Feedback

Feedback reveals whether or not you want to chat about a subject and whether the other person finds it intriguing. However, the major objective is to determine whether your claims are accurate or if they need to be rephrased.

You can learn the majority of the other person's ideas in this method. Only if it agrees with the claims needs to be acknowledged. If you give it some thought, you can circle the information you need and remove the irrelevant information. The circles then get progressively smaller until you reach the core.

You must confirm each indication of agreement, no matter how tiny, from the interlocutor and keep embellishing the remark by reframing it and repeating it. This provides the other person in the conversation with the impression that they are certain of their position and are thinking clearly.

The confirmation can be started with the words listed below: That is exactly what I meant, I confirm.
"That's the reason I," "So I assumed that," That explains the reason, "That implies..." This implies...

However, one cannot just restate the claim afterward. It's crucial to avoid saying everything that has already been stated. The impact is increased even further if you keep your remarks to the crucial points that are pertinent to the other person and the discussion's objective. The confirmation should be delivered in an easy-to-understand way.

In contrast, if the opposing side suggests that the statement is untrue, turn around and try again. Picking up your response and your words increases the strike rate while demonstrating empathy. The way the sentence was originally phrased also has an impact on this. Later on, we'll go into more detail about other ways to react to a failure. Flips remain unnoticeable if you respond to the opposing person's response swiftly and honestly. If you're successful, fishing is a fantastic weapon that may be used to get excellent hits in a variety of circumstances.

Returning to the earlier illustration "I get the impression that you aren't content yet." Yes, I'm truly satisfied, but I'm not sure what my wife would say about it if the interviewer could respond. Although it wasn't a definite hit, I wasn't entirely off either. I finally understood that he was considering something. He corrected it himself right away and informed me how important his wife's opinion is to him.

This indicates that I can utilize this knowledge to start the next conversation by saying, "This means that you value your wife's viewpoint in this situation." The comments also have another advantage. You discover the discrepancies between what you think and what the other person believes, and you discover how the other person interpreted the statement that you made for yourself.

Because you frequently say more than what the other person hears. Therefore, his method of interpretation is a crucial source of knowledge.

The other person's response can also demonstrate that the speaker's words do not line up with his body language, gestures, or speech. Imagine, for instance, that a manager replies to one of his employees because he believes that his workers are having issues with one another. But he refuses to discuss it, much less acknowledge that there is an issue at all. He reassures his employer that nothing is wrong and that there is no need for him to be concerned. His nonverbal communication indicates that the boss may be right about something. If he recognizes these signals, he can follow up and become more concrete.

Querying strategies

Some individuals believe that a mentalist never needs to speak up since he can hear what his opponent is thinking.

However, a mentalist's arsenal also includes several interrogation strategies that give off precisely this appearance. Asking for information should be as simple as that, right? No, there are methods to phrase inquiries so that the respondent understands them as statements rather than questions.

You can give the other personal information in this way that you could not possibly know yourself. You have the chance to carefully approach subjects or difficulties by answering hidden questions. In this manner, you can learn what the other person genuinely wants and believes without making them feel questioned or poked.

I struck up a conversation with a stranger at a function. I asked one of the following questions during the conversation. He was shocked since it seemed as though I knew he was self-employed without explicitly asking him. The man wanted to know immediately how I knew that.

He felt understood, and as a result, his attention was aroused and we had a wonderful talk. What kinds of questions are useful right now? The straight inquiry, the simplest method of gathering information is to ask the other person directly. For instance, you might ask the individual across from you, "Are you married?" if you want to know. This kind of questioning appears simple and apparent at first.

However, if they are timed correctly, direct questions can cause the other person to forget what was said. This typically occurs when there is some lag time between the question and the usage of the response and another topic is brought up.

One benefit of speaking with someone on the phone for business is that nobody expects you to be able to read their mind. Therefore, you have two choices: The best case scenario is that your question is forgotten by the other person in the conversation, and curiosity about what you know grows. You are still a very excellent listener, though, if the other person recalls the earlier query. They establish trust while expressing curiosity.

You can also get the other person to make important decisions by asking them directly. A person is likely to block you and say something like, "Sorry, but I don't have the time," if you approach them and bombard them with information right away. By obtaining a fundamental agreement beforehand, you can prevent this. Most people will either agree when you first ask if you may briefly explain something or inquire as to its subject. Asking for a less expensive time is always an option if it genuinely doesn't work. However, once you accept, there is no turning back. You have all the time you need to tell. The word "short" is also to blame for this. How much time is short? How long is it—a few seconds, five minutes, or thirty minutes? Short is a relative term that allows you the time you require.

If you want to deliver a quick story, this strategy has shown to be especially helpful. Authentic short stories are already quite good at communicating. The best way to achieve good communication would then be to ask, "May I short tell you a story?"

The casual inquiry

Direct queries stand out more than casual ones do. They typically take the form of brief statements that wrap up broader statements or sentences. Because of this, they have a secondary impact and get lost in the comments, especially when the question is posed with a hushed voice.

There are two types of casual questions used by mentalists. To determine how well you did with the previous assertion, feedback is necessary. Such banal inquiries may seem as follows: "... Is not it?"
Do you think that applies to you?
"Is this possible?"
Do you think that makes sense?
"Would you concur?"
Do you think that suits you?
"Is that accurate?"
"... Is that how you usually act?"
Is that connected to you?

The second type of informal question takes a step further and includes inquiries about who, what, where, when, how, and/or why. The casual question is again tacked on to the end of the remarks in this case.

The queries are phrased as follows this time: "... what may that signify for you?"

When did that happen to you?

Where could that possibly be?

"How on earth can you think that?"

Why does that apply to you, exactly?

As I already stated, the tone is crucial. The perception of the question's importance decreases the more casual it sounds. Everyone can convince his or her rival that he or she has only perception.

The covert query

When asking a question of this nature, a conjecture is used to form the question. You appear to be giving the person you are speaking to information with care. In actuality, the situation is reversed.

Consequently, this method is very efficient. This will be made clear with a brief example. Does your job require a lot of travel? This information can be hidden by saying something like, "It's just an idea, but I can imagine that you travel a lot and travel a lot... I think you do it as a result of your employment.

Every question can then be phrased in this manner as if you were making a statement. If the other party can concur, the assumption is right away assessed as a hit. There are methods to get out of the situation and make the statement into a hit if he disagrees. Extending the sentence in multiple directions can help you create the question. The person having the conversation typically indicates quickly which of the suggested interpretations apply to him using body language, gestures, facial expressions, or words.

The sentence "It may not be your current job, either; it is about former employment or a period in your life" can now be added to the example above. Perhaps your definition of travel is quite different from mine…

Pauses should be taken in between phrases to provide the listener time to respond. The success of this strategy depends on the appropriate timing. The accent is equally crucial. By slightly raising your voice at the end of a sentence, you can make it sound like a question. The voice must be reduced at the end of a sentence, the speaking rate must be slowed down, and a pause must then be made for the sentence to remark. As a result, the other person will interpret the query as a statement while also unconsciously inducing a response.

The citation query

This method is frequently used by card readers. The question is written as a statement in this instance as well. It is, however, also justified. A reference for the assertion is sought after. It serves as a reference system for a fortune teller who reads cards and makes statements like, "I see the map with the sword here. This typically indicates that there is a significant hurdle to be overcome. There may be a problem with someone nearby as well. Your problem may be professional rather than personal. How would you elucidate that?

What the sword means is of no relevance to the card reader. It makes no difference. It merely needs to be expressed with absolute conviction and sound plausible. The other person believes in the card's system of interpretation and thinks about how much the remark pertains to him. The card reader just inquired as to whether there were any current personal or professional issues.

Cards are not spread out and the discussion partner is not read out of the hand when communicating in business. However, this method can be used in regular conversational settings. The inquiry about work-related or personal issues would then sound like this: "I recently read something fascinating. Researchers have looked into how people are impacted by economic crises. Problems at work frequently spill over into personal life and vice versa. Some people are particularly terrified about being demoted. What do you make of it? The tarot card is no longer my reference; I now use scientists.

I'm not sure if studies on the aforementioned issue exist. It is also wholly immaterial because the remark is understood to be true simply by the sentence "Scientists have found that..." The majority of individuals think that everything a scientist, researcher, or expert says is true. Belief in the accuracy of the reference in question is the deciding element.

The popular query
Whether the other person agrees or disagrees with the questioning strategy is irrelevant. You're always correct, it is a perfect technique that, after being mastered and honed, is quite powerful. The intended question is posed in an unclear manner. The inquiry is asked in the

negative, which is odd. The question is then rephrased but without a negative. At first, this might seem a little unusual and difficult, but when implemented, it works incredibly well. The example that follows will demonstrate this.

You're not working for yourself, are you?
Depending on his response right now, you could answer the question in the following manner:
First possibility: I'm not a self-employed person.
"Just as I suspected," was the reply.
Second possibility: I do work for myself.
"Yes, I believe so," was the reply.

The person on the other side will typically only recall the portion of the question that applies to him when using this kind of inquiry because both options are always kept open. A mentalist would do the following to further sidestep the question and obfuscate the ambiguity: he would support his claims with additional ones that made sense with the overall message.

Using the aforementioned case once more
You're not working for yourself, are you?
First possibility: I'm not a self-employed person.
"Just as I suspected," was the reply.
Confirmation: I find it hard to believe you would want to put up with the anxiety and rage that comes with being a business owner. They place a higher value on having stable work with a set wage.

Second possibility: I do work for myself.

"Yes, I believe so," was the reply.

Confirmation: I find it hard to believe that you would enjoy being bossed around. You want to work for yourself and engage in a fulfilling endeavor. You must be very talented and motivated to put good ideas into practice.

In actual use, the hit-question method is quite successful. It works especially effectively if you have a creative mind and can think of supporting arguments on the spot. It is important to have a few potential comments prepared in advance if you plan to utilize this asking approach often in the same situation.

Gathering information

A clairvoyant by the name of Hanussen created a lot of commotion in Berlin in the 1930s with his protests and forecasts. He provided countless private audiences where he predicted the future of people in addition to his well-paid performances in the Varieté Scala, which is well-known throughout Germany. He had prepared a lavish apartment for this purpose, which was accessed through a cryptic anteroom. The visitors were then welcomed by enigmatic secretaries in the next two antechambers.

You weren't allowed to see the medium Hanussen until after another waiting period. In reality, he was incredibly knowledgeable about his clients. Everything from living circumstances to special occasions to individual preferences. Superhuman abilities? Scam? Understanding of human nature? Or a combination of the two?

This can be explained easily. The visitor was to be questioned by the two secretaries from the vestibules. Everything that might be significant for the Master's prophecies caught their attention. The assistant had to call for more information while the visitor waited in the second room. Hanussen paid dearly for his prophecies, and all the material was given to the clairvoyant, who then presented his information as if he had received it from another realm. And if he hadn't been killed by the SA in April 1933—the reasons for the assassination have not yet been definitively established—someone would have discovered his lie very quickly.

Hanussen used comparable techniques in the mental displays of the variety shows at the time, if you set aside his esoteric humbug and his scams and just examine his methods. You enter z. For instance, in a newspaper ad that sought out individuals with a particular interest in the paranormal even though it seems unbelievable, many believers reacted. Each person was engaged in discussion by an intermediary who was gathering data. The mentalist then invited the audience to a specific presentation.

The latter then asked the chosen individuals to take the stage during the performance, and when they did, the audience was in awe as he reportedly read their minds as revealed the previously acquired information. Even the test subject himself was frequently astounded by the mentalist's level of familiarity with him because, due to the manner he had been questioned previously, he had not even registered what he was saying.

Another strategy involved hanging a photograph of the mentalist from the variety show next to the bathroom mirror. Before his show, the mentalist himself barricaded himself in a booth and overheard the women talking. They were prompted to discuss the upcoming mentalist concert by the poster. They also discussed personal information, which gave the presentation a strong framework for mind reading.

In conclusion, it should be mentioned that the success of these miracles depends on the more or less skillful acquisition of the necessary knowledge when viewed objectively from the outside. Additionally, the speakers had sufficient empathy and understanding of human nature to address the audience and discuss their desires.

What information does this give us? Additionally, having the right knowledge and being well-prepared is crucial for our business communications. Some people show up unprepared for a job interview and then wonder why they don't obtain the position they want. And in crucial discussions, which frequently involve large sums of money, you frequently promote your concept rather than addressing the real factors that led to the other party's choice. In conclusion, you should spend more time preparing for key conversations.

The first step is to ask yourself, "What can I anticipate?" You will be better able to respond in conversation if you ask yourself this question and try to imagine yourself in the conversation. While in the 1920s and 1930s mentalists still needed to put in a lot of work and hire workers, getting information today is much simpler because of the Internet.

Many people participate in social networks, post images and videos there, and even keep a wish list of items they want to buy at the online store Amazon. We post a ton of material on a variety of websites without always realizing that it is also accessible to the general public. On Facebook, every one may see your name and profile picture. If you are listed in the phone book, your information will also be available online.

Forum posts are typically viewable and available to everyone. You can acquire a thorough description of the person if you combine this information intelligently.

The first route takes you to Google. Typically, you get the initial hits here. These search engines' ability to categorize all results is an advantage. For instance, a bundle of images from Wikipedia or social media sites is displayed. The collection of phone numbers from online phone books falls under a different category. Additionally, email addresses are shown. Otherwise, Google would merely contain a disorganized list of them. The list also includes blogs and website hits.

The example that follows demonstrates how effective online research may be. Say you want to schedule a meeting with Mr. Walter K. His name came up in a social network during the initial search. Although Walter K. placed restrictions on the release of his content, his name, profile photo, and email address are still visible.

Additional information is available on a site for business connections. His hobbies are listed below along with his present employer and prior employers. World travel is something Walter K. enjoys. A quick search on

Amazon's wish lists reveals that he enjoys classical music and is curious about video editing. He also has a new video camera on his wish list.

The internet directory search then goes on. Here are the listings from the printed phone books. His precise address is provided to us, which connects us to Google Maps or another map provider. We can even practically visit his family's home on the outskirts of Munich thanks to Street View. The opulent off-road vehicle in the driveway not only reveals the make and model of the vehicle he is driving but also suggests that he is probably not exactly indigent.

In the Google search results, his name is included on a home association website. You can read there that Walter K. moved to Munich seven years ago for work-related reasons and that he remains dedicated to the team. Walter K. is active on Twitter and occasionally tweets about his travels, according to more research. Searching for his Twitter handle takes you to a forum where he occasionally contributes. He recently declared his excitement about a trip to the Grand Canyon.

His blog is the next. He highlights some of his travels' high points here. The Flickr photo service hosts pictures.

You can infer a lot of things about Walter K. from this information. He drives a black Range Rover and resides in Munich.

He enjoys visiting different locations and documenting his experiences in pictures and movies. His preferred musical genre is classical. His Xing posts demonstrate that he has been working for himself for twelve years.

Walter K. is devoted to his community and participates in charity events as a member of the established club. He's going to the Grand Canyon soon.

The experiment below, conducted by a film crew in Brussels, demonstrates how well such research performs. In a common area, it had erected a huge white tent. There was a purported clairvoyant inside. Now, many passersby were approached and asked to judge this miracle worker's abilities. A few onlookers concurred, and the performance began.

Each subject entered the tent on their own. There were two chairs and a sizable table inside. The color scheme was preserved to white. The clairvoyant appeared quite enigmatic and was also clothed in white. This staging contributed to the overall mystique of the situation.
The subject was greeted, seated down, and the clairvoyant started the procedure of summoning before reading his counterpart's thoughts.

The volunteer's hometown, school, and best friend's name might all be disclosed. He could even explain his house and his bank information. From the expressions of the participants, it was clear how impressive it was to them. Everything was eventually disassembled. Several others could be seen looking up information on the topics on the Internet as a white curtain collapsed. In summary, it is now feasible to swiftly find high-quality information about a conversation partner online with a few clicks. In the era of smartphones and portable tablet PCs, everywhere, anytime, everyone.

Statistics and surveys, which are published in newspapers or can be obtained in online databases, are another source of information. A variety of information is available from the Federal Statistical Office. In such databases, you can also search for details regarding the standard of living in a certain area. Discussions can benefit from this information. Additionally, businesses self-report customer data and statistically assess them.

For instance, Amazon keeps track of the things you have purchased and those you are browsing for. Amazon then presents the products that would be of interest to the user based on this. Customer surveys are another alternative. This makes it possible for businesses to ascertain the preferences of many of their clients. If the surveys are tailored to each respondent, you will receive unique information that may be skillfully incorporated into the following client interaction.

In business, competition is frequently used to acquire data. You must fill out a card with your name and address if you wish to enter the raffle. A personal follow-up inquiry is typically asked. You now have the chance to target potential customers.

The waiting area, secretary's anteroom, and reception areas are all excellent places to observe individuals. Therefore, the reception employees must have excellent people skills. This process could be viewed critically. The reality is that a large number of people have voluntarily supplied personal information.

Additionally, the objective of the information's utilization should be taken into account. They will also have an interest if the knowledge is applied to help them respond to the interlocutor more effectively.

Analyze feelings

Our lives revolve around our emotions. They have an impact on how we think and behave. We frequently act in ways that are not informed by reason but rather by feelings. Only after that do we search, consciously or unconsciously, for a rationale for our behavior. Because we don't always trust our emotions, there are occasions when we don't realize they have led us. We use our moods to intentionally and unconsciously communicate our thoughts. We exhibit responses to what we go through. Knowing how the other person is feeling at this moment will help you get a better understanding of their ideas.

Paul Ekman, an anthropologist, and psychologist from the United States is renowned for his studies on nonverbal cues and is regarded as a pioneer in the field of in-depth face analysis. To discern emotional expression patterns in the face of his counterpart, he created the Facial Action Coding System. He has traversed the globe to look at how people communicate their emotions.

According to his ethnological research, everyone in the globe experiences the same seven basic emotions, regardless of where they are from or what culture they are a part of.

- Shock
- Anxiety
- Grief and despair

- Contempt
- Disgust
- Anger, anger, and more anger
- Joy

Below, the specific emotional states are described in more detail. In practice, the signals are less overt and only sometimes displayed in their most extreme state. These straightforward instructions are very significant. The tiny shifts in the other person's face can give you a hint as to what they were thinking instead of saying.

Three subtle facial expressions are distinguished by Paul Ekman: the weak expression, the partial expression, and the micro-expression. When the emotion first appears, it is barely felt and the expression is feeble. However, as the emotion increases in intensity, the facial expression does too, becoming less subtly more obvious, and stronger. Your facial expression will be weak if you attempt to suppress emotion and the signals that go along with it, especially if you are not very successful. The weak facial expression can only be seen in a small portion of the face, whereas the partial expression is only partially developed.

The micro print normally appears extremely rapidly and vanishes without warning. A fifth of a second is all that it is visible for. You risk missing this crucial advice if you are not paying attention right now. Micro prints can cover the entire face or just a portion of it, making identification more challenging. However, it is attainable with training. The micro expression happens when you are feeling something but are hiding it out of concern for other people. However, it can also happen when a person is unsure about their own emotions, i.e., when they are unsure of what they are feeling. Then the emotion is unconsciously expressed.

Surprise

You'll be startled if something occurs that you didn't anticipate. You can't prepare for a surprise, so you can't suppress this feeling either. Since surprise only lasts for a brief period, it is only briefly visible on the discussion partner's face. The surprise normally gives way to another emotion as soon as you comprehend what is happening. There is no requirement to feel the way that you do, though. When the event that caused the surprise has no repercussions, this is the case.

Surprise is not the same as fear. The latter is an involuntary reflex that causes us to crouch and squeeze our faces. On the other hand, the surprise is defined by a wide-open expression on the face. Because surprised people raise their eyebrows dramatically, you can tell when someone is astonished. As a result, there is more skin showing beneath the brows and on the forehead's horizontal lines. Even in a calm, emotion-free state, wrinkles that are already present deepen.

The lower portion of the face also shows reactions. The mouth opens as the lower jaw drops. The wider the mouth expands, the bigger the surprise. There are a few key factors to take into account to distinguish genuine astonishment from other emotions. You can conclude that the surprise has been played if it is displayed for an excessively long time.

No surprise is displayed if only the lips open but the eyebrows are still. Simply put, the guy is speechless. When the mouth remains closed and only the eyebrows are elevated, there is uncertainty. The eyes alone can convey increased curiosity and a desire to exclaim "wow" if they are wide open.

Anxiety

If you find yourself in a precarious scenario when bodily harm or psychological harm is at stake, you start to panic. When you are afraid, all you can think about is yourself and feel your fear. Everything is centered on it. This keeps happening until the threat has passed. Panic sets in if the threat is still present.

We live with fears the entire time. For thousands of years, they have been biologically developed in our brains. Reflexively fleeing or becoming paralyzed with terror are examples of anxiety reactions. Additionally, evolution can be used to explain the latter. Our forefathers had to defend themselves from invading forces. However, a lot of predators don't see their prey until it moves. Therefore, freezing was a means of surviving.

But dread is not merely an antiquated byproduct of evolution. Quite the opposite. The sensation continues to have a protective purpose. We are cautioned and made vigilant by fear. It stops the careless activity and shields us from harm.

The startling facial reactions reveal the presence of terror. Although elevated, the eyebrows are still straight. This lifting occurs somewhat less forcefully than the emotion of astonishment. Along with being brought together, the inner ends of the eyebrows also move closer than when the emotion of surprise is present.

The forehead may also have a few fine lines. The rigidity and vast openness of the eyes make it easy to see the white of the eye. The lips are pursed and slightly pulled back. Even if the other person tries to disguise their anxiety, it is clear if their lips are merely curled in terror. The opposing party is worried if the only signs of anxiety are raised eyebrows.

Angst and despondency

There is no muscle tension in the face of a griever. Whenever we lose someone or anything, we essentially experience the emotion of grief in varying degrees of intensity. For instance, you may be in a desperate situation and feel alone if a good friend suddenly stops communicating with you. You are likely sad and disappointed if an anticipated event does not happen. Or perhaps something doesn't function the way you'd like it to, leaving you feeling helpless. We typically withdraw or become irate as a result.

We respond to this emotion differently depending on the circumstance and our attitude. The eyebrows are the finest facial feature to identify sadness. The brows furrow and lift a little above the bridge of the nose. The eyebrows are slightly slanted because the outer ends are not aligned. Small, vertical wrinkles between the brows are now very noticeable. Additionally pulled up are the upper eyelid's inner folds. As a result, a triangular shape is produced, which stands out, especially for the fundamental emotion of mourning.

The triangle, which also appears when the inner section of the eyebrows is only slightly lifted, is the most crucial sign of mourning. The lower eyelid also tenses up when the grief is extremely intense. The corners of the mouth slant downward and slightly form an inverted U in the lower portion of the face. Most of the time, the lower lip is also pulled forward, creating a pout. The chin's skin has a small curve to it. The vision is frequently unfocused and vacant.

Disgust

You avoid something if you find it repulsive. This is the exact aim of distaste. From a biological perspective, it ought to indicate that something is harmful to us and that we ought to avoid it. The normal disgust-inducing odor, taste, or touch is unpleasant. All it takes is a notion to make us feel revulsion.

When you feel revulsion at the sight of a particular individual, your empathy and, consequently, your social behavior are affected. When adults observe a child engaging in morally repugnant activity, they frequently feel horrified.

The upper lip is raised and the nose wrinkles when someone feels disgusted. The upper lip is pulled back against the little forward movement of the lower lip. Above and near the nose, wrinkles are visible. These lines become progressively more visible as the disdain grows.

Additionally elevated are the cheeks, which lift the lower eyelids. The eyes now appear smaller and the area surrounding the eyes develops more creases. The brows are slightly lowered. When the head tilts back or to the side, you should maintain your distance from the person. Because the forehead and brows are little engaged in the expression of disgust, it is simple to mimic it. Therefore, you cannot determine if the revulsion is genuine. It is also challenging to conceal disgust. Even if you aren't aware of it, your nose will wrinkle if you grin while feeling a bit disgusted.

Contempt

In terms of emotional psychology, contempt is a feeling that is made up of disgust and rage. Nevertheless, it is acknowledged as its own fundamental emotion by a variety of emotion experts. Contempt, in its most extreme manifestation, is the evaluation of others as inferior and a sense of superiority toward them. If a person of higher social standing believes that those of lower status are inferior, contempt can spread from top to bottom. Such a case would be a department head who feels that his staff "is not getting anything done anyway."

Contempt can also rise from the bottom up, for instance, if the staff feels the manager hasn't even earned the right to be there. Contempt is characterized by the mouth. You appear to be trying to smile because the corner of your mouth is tense and slightly pulled up. However, it's also possible that the upper lip is only pulled up on one side. The more the upper lip or mouth corner lifts, the more contemptuous the expression. Often, a tiny jerky exhales via the nostrils is another feature of this emotion. The gaze typically casts the despised person in a demeaning light, but contempt takes precedence.

Anger, anger, and anger

When we are prevented from performing any action, we experience anger. This can occur if someone stands in our way or if something does not function as planned. Violence and threats of violence are additional sources of rage. Anger is not only directed at other people or objects; it can also be directed at oneself. It is the most harmful of the basic emotions, as it increases the likelihood of verbally or physically harming one's partner.

Anger in its purest form is short-lived, as it rapidly combines with fear or disdain. The eyebrows are brought together and lowered when one is irritated. This results in vertical creases between the eyebrows. The forehead is wrinkle-free. The eyes are locked on the opposing individual with a piercing glance. The greater the elevation of the lower eyelid, the greater the fury.

The pupils become smaller. Typically, the mouth is shut and the lips are squeezed together. Also possible is an open mouth, as if shouting at someone. Frequently, pressed lips are the first symptom of fury. If you discover this suggestion directed at the other individual, he may be unaware of his reaction. However, if only the eyebrows are brought together and the mouth remains unchanged, this indicates greater focus. You may be certain that the person you're conversing with is angry only when the lips and eye region both exhibit indicators of rage.

Joy

Joy is the only good emotion. A condition of contentment that we are all likely pursuing. You constantly feel joy when something that makes you joyful occurs, such as achieving the desired goal or being in the company of someone you adore.

You can tell if someone is truly joyful or just pretending. We frequently have an innate ability to distinguish between a genuine and a fake smile. The latter appears largely unnatural and artificial. Often, phony enthusiasm can be detected in the voice.

Two major facial muscles are utilized for a genuine smile. One ensures that the mouth's corners are raised. The eye region contracts through the other. The skin beneath the eyelids contracts, and the eyebrows descend. Small smile lines emerge around the eyes. Due to the uncontrollable nature of this mechanism, it is particularly clear if the delight is genuine or phony. Only the corners of the lips can be affected consciously. The only thing that makes a smile genuine are the fine lines generated by the tightening of the skin around the eyes.

Utilize facial expression data

If you are presented with emotions during a conversation, you should first investigate their origins. To accomplish this, evaluate the surrounding circumstances. If the emotion has existed since the beginning of the talk, it is conceivable that it has nothing to do with the current circumstance. Much more probable, the emotion was prompted by an occurrence that occurred before the talk. Or, the partner's expectations for the dialogue are expressed through this emotion. If you are aware of this, resolving potential objections and reservations and meeting positive expectations will be easy.

With grief, wrath, fear, disgust, and contempt, one should attempt to prevent the sensation from entirely spreading to the other individual. You should respond to even subtle cues by deftly addressing your opponent. Surprise is unique in that it can be either positive or unpleasant. The delight, on the other hand, can only benefit the dialogue because it has a favorable effect on the circumstance as a whole.

If you identify terror on your counterpart's face, you do not first know what it is scared of. It would be ideal if that could be deduced solely from facial expressions. But you must consider the entire situation. If the interlocutor is tense before the conversation, he may be anticipating negative news. Or he attempts to conceal something and fears being discovered. If you have doubts, you should attempt to make the other person feel secure. Now, it is essential to investigate the situation thoroughly. Such a statement may be, "I have the impression that you are experiencing great difficulty with something." If you suspect that there is more to the story or that something you should know is being concealed, you can respond by saying, "I believe there is something else we should discuss. There is a good chance that the person you are speaking with may initiate a conversation.

The most significant aspect of discovering signs of mourning is to take them seriously. How you react to grief in particular relies on the nature of your relationship with the deceased. In any event, the individual should be permitted to withdraw. You may also offer a chat if you thoroughly assess the situation.

Possible opening line: "I have the feeling that something is wrong." However, this approach depends heavily on whether you are the appropriate person with whom the other person wishes to discuss your pain. It is uncertain whether an employee desires consolation from his supervisor. Perhaps a coworker or a friend is the best option here. As previously stated, it is crucial to go gently and carefully. Better talk less and listen more. When the opposite side is ready, it reveals the situation on its own.

Also, you can react to distaste. Have you observed something repulsive with the other person, such as B. rotten food, for example? If so, you should immediately address the other person's thoughts. If the opponent's disdain is focused on a specific individual, the observation should not be explicitly addressed. Depending on the situation, if one has a suspicion about the trigger, one may question carefully or formulate an ambiguous statement. But if you immediately address the emotion, it will typically intensify.

The other individual's contempt for us may be directed toward itself, something else, or itself. If the latter is true, it is usually advisable to do nothing and ignore this individual. She may feel superior to us for whatever reason. Other explanations may be gleaned from this situation.

If the signals oscillate between disdain and rage, it is possible that the other person does not know what he is feeling. The emotion may just be beginning to develop. Now, as with other emotions, it is essential to demonstrate empathy. You can attempt to learn more about the cause and potentially alleviate the emotion. However, the individual should never be surrounded.

If you observe symptoms of rage on the other person's face, you should proceed with extreme caution. Perhaps it is only the intense gaze that resembles rage. Otherwise, the question of who and why the individual is upset emerges. Assume the employer has just fired an employee and detects the initial signals of rage. Therefore, the emotion is just emerging. The question remains whether the worker is angry with himself or with the manager. Does he become enraged because he believes he could have done his job better and avoided being fired? Or is he unhappy with his boss because he knows he cannot provide for his family if he loses his job?

Therefore, you should reconsider the circumstances and determine why he is angry. How should you respond if it turns out that the employee's hostility is directed at the supervisor? If you inquired, "Are you angry?" There is a strong likelihood that the fury will intensify. It is more intelligent to feel and examine your surroundings. Instead of a clumsy response, empathy could be demonstrated: »I realize that you are currently disturbed. I apologize or I would have reacted in the same way. In this circumstance, more assistance can be provided.

If you observe happiness on the other person's face, this is typically not an issue. On the contrary, it is advantageous and desirable to understand what pleases and elicits positive emotions in the other person. If the dialogue allows you to return to this point, you can maintain a cheerful mood or restore it in difficult situations. For instance, if you begin by discussing your partner's previous vacation, you can return to the topic if it's appropriate and reignite the related positive mood.

Typically, the emotion of surprise is followed by another, indicating that the most recent event has been processed. The following feeling explains the genuine emotional state to which you must react. If it is contextually appropriate to reflect on the other person's thinking and strengthen the connection of trust, one may add, "You are probably shocked." For instance, when a supervisor informs an employee of a promotion, the person's countenance may initially express astonishment and then, after a few moments, happiness.

Now the boss says something like, "I know it's unexpected." But I had previously assumed that you would be pleased, » he says, expressing what the employee has just observed and his ideas.

Chapter Five

CONCLUSION

You now understand the secrets of mind hacking. This book contains all the pertinent information regarding it. You may have been first fascinated and apprehensive about the possibility of peering into the minds of others. However, you may already be considering how to use what you have read, or you may have even attempted it. In this way, you have determined the significant influence that Mind Hacking can have.

Professionals employ the tools and strategies presented in this book to decipher people's thoughts. You were able to convince yourself that mind hacking is not supernatural, but rather based on detailed observation of your opponent, knowledge of human nature, and reliance on past experiences. In this regard, genuine mentalists differ from magicians. The latter performs primarily magic feats.

Everyone can employ these mental communication techniques. However, one thing is crucial. You must have a genuine interest in your counterpart. Only then can you truly comprehend the other's mental universe?